JOHN GILMARY SHEA

JOHN GILMARY SHEA

JOHN GILMARY SHEA

Father of American Catholic History

1824-1892

by

PETER GUILDAY

REPRINTED FROM
RECORDS AND STUDIES
JULY, 1926

4979

NEW YORK
THE UNITED STATES
CATHOLIC HISTORICAL SOCIETY
1926

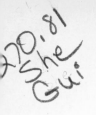

CONTENTS

ILLUSTRATIONS

PREFACE

Several short biographical notices of the scholar, upon whom the present generation has bestowed the unique title, Father of American Catholic History, have appeared since the death of John Gilmary Shea on February 22, 1892. Among these are: a sketch written by his daughter at the time of the Georgetown College Centenary (1889) for a Catholic weekly, the *Century,* then published in Washington, D. C.; one written for the *Ave Maria* by the late Maurice Francis Egan in 1892; another by Shea's friend, Marc F. Vallette, which appeared in the *Catholic World* in 1892; one published by Richard F. Clarke in the *Catholic Family Almanac* of 1893; and a biographical notice appended to the new edition of Shea's translation of Le Clercq's *Establishment of the Faith* (1901).

The only adequate account of John Gilmary Shea's life and works is the tribute paid by Dr. James J. Walsh which appeared in the *American Catholic Quarterly Review* for April, 1913. This is based upon Dr. Walsh's speech at the unveiling of the Shea Memorial Tablet at the Newark Cathedral, October 12, 1912.

Thirty-four years have passed since John Gilmary Shea finished his labors in the field of Catholic historical scholarship. During that time his place in the history of American Catholicism has grown in importance with all who realize how much we depend upon his researches for our knowledge of the past.

He was above all a man of devotion to the Catholic Faith. He stood out among the men of erudition of his time. He was a model husband, a loving father, and a constant companion to his children.

Some time ago, through the gracious kindness of his only surviving daughter, Dr. Shea's personal correspondence and private papers were placed in my care in order to ensure their preservation. I need not say with what reverence I have read these intimate glimpses into his life and labors and especially into his sorrows.

The sketch given in these pages is hardly a biography; in fact a biography of Dr. Shea would be difficult. His was a life almost of the cloister. For years he was editor of three magazines in which his name never appeared; and although during the later years of his life, another editorial position brought him before the Catholic public, he never mingled in the affairs of men to such an extent as to have a lasting influence upon them. Quiet, shy, retiring, unobtrusive, with a degree of humility rare for one who had been so successful in his chosen field, his was a life with the past rather than with the present.

The bibliography of Shea's works in the appendix is based upon the catalogue published by the Rev. Edward P. Spillane, S.J., in the *Historical Records and Studies*.

All who have written in the field of American Catholic history since Shea's death have been proud to admit their dependence upon his scholarly studies. It is to the nascent school of young Catholic historians in the United States that these pages are offered as a means of inspiration and as a tribute to a master.

PETER GUILDAY.

December 8, 1925.

JOHN GILMARY SHEA

CHAPTER I

Boyhood

(1824—1838)

In a *Pastoral Address* to the congregation at St. Patrick's
Cathedral, dated February 20, 1838, and signed by Bishop Dubois, of New York, the causes of the conflict between ecclesiastical authority and the trustees are sternly reviewed and the
thorny question of jurisdiction over the temporalities of the diocese is challenged to a final issue. This remarkable document
is wrongly dated. It was written by John Hughes, who had
been consecrated coadjutor-Bishop of New York on January
7, 1838. The date, then, is probably February 20, 1839.

Shortly after the consecration of his coadjutor, Bishop Dubois
transferred to Bishop Hughes the administration of the temporal
affairs of the diocese, reserving all spiritual jurisdiction to himself. In January 21, 1838, Bishop Dubois solemnly dedicated
St. Paul's Church, Brooklyn, the site of which was the gift of
Cornelius Heeney. A few days afterwards, Bishop Dubois was
stricken with paralysis. Two other attacks followed within the
next four months, and it was evident to everyone, except to the
venerable bishop himself, that the temporary peace occasioned
by the consecration of his coadjutor would be seriously threatened
if he were to insist upon ruling the diocese in his impaired condition.

The situation was an unfortunate one. During the first year
of his coadjutorship, Bishop Hughes refrained from taking a
stand against the misrule which had hindered spiritual progress

9

in the diocese for over a decade, lest Dr. Dubois, who was then seventy-five years old, should regard it as an invasion of his episcopal rights. Another factor was present in the confused situation at the Cathedral. The pastor of the Cathedral, Father Thomas Levins, had attacked Father Hughes in the *Truth Teller,* over the signature "Fergus McAlpin," and the bitter personal controversy which followed, was not forgotten when Dr. Hughes came to New York, as coadjutor-Bishop, eight years later.

Father Levins had been pastor of the Cathedral since the days of Bishop Connolly. During the earlier years of Bishop Dubois' episcopate, Father Levins' brusque and irascible temperament brought him into conflict with his superior. Though the difficulty between Bishop Dubois and the pastor of the Cathedral was not a very serious one, the question of obedience to lawful jurisdiction was involved. In 1834, Father Levins disrespectfully refused to obey Bishop Dubois and suspension followed. The trustees took up the cause of the suspended priest and five years later they openly rebelled against the authority of both bishops. On February 10, 1839, by order of the trustees, a constable expelled a teacher in the Cathedral Sunday school, who had been appointed by Dr. Dubois.

It was at this juncture that the *Pastoral* was issued. That a change had at last come in the history of the trustee system was evident to all who heard Bishop Hughes read the *Pastoral* on Sunday, February 24, 1839. The conflict was not over the rejection of young Leopold De Grandval, the teacher, who as a friend of Dr. Dubois was obnoxious to the trustees; it was over trusteeism itself. In language so clear and so forcible that there could be no misunderstanding his meaning, Bishop Hughes stigmatized the conduct of the trustees as insubordination to Church law. The law of the State gave to the trustees control over the church and the revenues; but no power could give laymen jurisdiction over the clergy and the Sacraments. They were told that they might do as they pleased with the building; but that, unless they acted in perfect conformity with the canon law of the Church, the priests would be withdrawn and the Cathedral laid under interdict. Whatever power the trustees possessed by the law of the State had been given them in order to aid religion, not to hinder it.

There is one passage towards the end of this document which has a particular interest for us. The *Pastoral* marks the initial stage of the end of the trustee system in the Diocese of New York. "Do not suppose," Bishop Hughes wrote, "that the Church of God, because she has no civil support for her laws and discipline, is therefore obliged to see them trampled on by her own children, without any means for their preservation. She has means; and it is necessary that her discipline be restored, and the abuses on the part of your trustees, to which we have alluded, be disavowed and removed."

To this hint of one fearsome sanction, the interdict, Bishop Hughes added another: that of excommunication. He warned the congregation that this weapon would be used against any member of the Board of Trustees who should hinder the vindication of the laws and discipline of the Church. "Are you satisfied," he says, "with the constitution, doctrine, and authority of the Catholic Church, as she has descended to us from Jesus Christ? Is it your wish that there shall be no innovations, no amendments derived from civil charters and secular laws? If so, meet in the vestry this afternoon, to record your support of the principles of your religion in their entire integrity. If any one is offended at your doing so, he need not attend. He is not a Catholic, or if he be, *he is not worthy to transmit to his children that faith* for which his forefathers gloriously encountered poverty and persecution in the land where the Church was loved, and the Faith preserved at the sacrifice of all besides. For him the house of God has no comeliness. For his eye, the tabernacles of Jacob and the tents of Israel have no beauty. The integrity and miraculous unity of the Church spread over all the earth, and yet realizing the figure of one sheepfold and one shepherd, even this idea can excite no rapture in his breast. Let him go:—*he is the last of a faithful line, but that Faith of his ancestors shall die with him, and his family shall furnish no heir to the inheritance of spiritual life.* But is there such a one among *you*, dearly beloved brethren?"

To none among those present was this dire prophecy directed more particularly than to a leader of the trustees of the day, James Shea, the father of John Gilmary Shea.

Young Shea's boyhood was passed in the midst of the acri-

monious disputes between Bishop Dubois and the trustees, and
there is a pathetic note written in his own hand on the last page
of the pastoral many years later, when James Shea's son was acknowledged as the historian of the Catholic Church in the United
States: "I hope I have repaired any scandal he gave and have
shown myself zealously obedient in matters of faith and discipline."

James Shea belonged to an interesting group of Irishmen who
had established themselves in New York during the closing years
of the eighteenth century and the first two decades of the nine-
teenth century. Leaders at the time among these cultured laymen were Andrew Morris, Francis Cooper, Cornelius Heeney,
John George Gottsberger, William James Macneven, Charles
O'Conor, Bernard Dornin, John Doyle, Matthew Field, Dominick
Lynch, Jr., George Pardow, William Denman, Thomas Brady,
Patrick Sarsfield Casserly, and many others, to whom the building up of the Church in New York in these early days was
mainly due.

James Shea was the son of Patrick and Mary (Real) Shea,
of Pallas Green, Ireland, where he was born in 1790. His parents were in comfortable circumstances and he received an excellent classical education. At the age of twenty-five he came to
the United States with the intention of studying medicine and
then of settling here permanently. The captain of the vessel on
which he sailed had treated his passengers so harshly during
the six weeks' voyage that he feared to land them at New York,
lest their Irish compatriots might demand redress. Accordingly,
he ran his ship up the Shrewsbury River and ordered the passengers off at a secluded spot near the Jersey coast.

James Shea arrived here with letters of introduction to prominent Irishmen and with sufficient funds to make a start towards
his chosen profession. Walking up the country road that pleasant morning in May, 1815, he saw a farmer ploughing in a nearby
field and stopped to ask for information how to reach New
York. The dinner gong sounded while they were talking, and
the farmer, who was General John A. Schuyler, a soldier of the
Revolutionary War, invited the young Irishman to dine with
him. At the table, another guest, a Protestant minister, began
an attack on the Church, and Shea answered his objections so

ST. PETER'S CHURCH, BARCLAY STREET, NEW YORK

cleverly and with so much good humor that General Schuyler took a fancy to him and offered him a place in the family circle as tutor to his sons and nephew.

Shea accepted, remaining with the Schuylers for several years. He then came to New York where he became a partner in the school of Eber Wheaton. By strict economy he had saved his original funds and had added to them from his pension as private tutor to the Schuylers. He had determined to earn sufficient for his daily needs by teaching and to expend his savings on the studies preparatory to a medical degree. Wheaton's school failed, and in the failure James Shea lost all his money. The next few years were spent in organizing a school of his own.

In 1820, James Shea married Mary Ann Flannigan, who was born in New York City, July 15, 1800. She was the daughter of Owen Flannigan and Ann McCurtin, and the granddaughter of Thomas and Deborah (Cox) McCurtin. Through her grandmother, Mrs. James Shea was a direct descendant of Nicholas Upsall, who came out to Massachusetts with Governor Winthrop in 1630, and whose genial figure is described in Longfellow's *New England Tragedies*. Thomas McCurtin, of Carringnavan, Ireland, emigrated to America in 1760, and settled in Mt. Holly, New Jersey, where he opened a school in 1762. Like so many of his countrymen, Thomas McCurtin received a thorough education in the classics and in the mathematical sciences. Deborah Cox, his wife, had been a student at the Ursuline Academy in New York City and was a devoted friend of Father Kohlmann, S.J., Bishop Cheverus, and Father Benedict Fenwick, S.J. One of Cheverus' gifts to her as a young girl was an *Ecce Homo,* said to be by Albrecht Dürer, now in the possession of Georgetown University. Mrs. McCurtin, from early youth, was devoted to the study of the Bible.

Their daughter, Ann, was born in Mt. Holly, in the year 1776. Mrs. McCurtin instilled a great love of the Holy Scriptures in her daughter's heart, and Ann McCurtin bequeathed this gift to her grandson, John Gilmary Shea, who was destined to revive interest in biblical studies among American Catholics. The McCurtins moved from Mt. Holly to Philadelphia after the War of Independence, in order to enjoy the advantages of their Faith, and both husband and wife were carried off in the epidemic of

1793, in which Bishop-elect Lawrence Graessel and Father Francis A. Fleming, O.P., died. Thomas McCurtin's brother, Daniel, fought in one of the Pennsylvania companies during the Revolution and is the author of a *Journal of the Times at the Siege of Boston and our Arrival at Cambridge near Boston, August 9, 1775.* Ann McCurtin married Owen Flannigan, of New York City, and it was their daughter, Mary Ann Flannigan, who became the mother of John Gilmary Shea.

James and Mary Ann (Flannigan) Shea had several children, two of them reached manhood: Charles Edward, who graduated with honors at Columbia College and who became a member of the New York bar; and John Dawson (Gilmary), who was born in New York City, on July 22, 1824, and was baptized by Father John Power, the pastor of old St. Peter's Church in Barclay Street.

John Gilmary Shea's genealogy is given as follows:

Thomas McCurtin [1793]   Deborah Cox [1793]

Patrick Shea   Mary Beal   Owen Flannigan   Ann McCurtin
Ireland   Ireland

James Real Shea [1790-1843]   Mary Ann Flannigan [1800-1841]

John Gilmary Shea [1824-1892]

James Shea was thirty years old at the time of his marriage. He had become one of the recognized leaders in the New York private schools. His own school in the Bowery lasted until 1829, when he was appointed head of the Department of English in what is now Columbia University. His pupils then entered the Columbia Grammar School. Like many of the Irishmen of his day, James Shea took an active part in politics, although he always refused to accept office. As a Sachem of Tammany, he was a recognized leader among his people, and his prominence in Catholic affairs increased owing to the interest he took in Catholic Emancipation, the Repeal Movement, the Irish Emigrant Society, and in the local militia, in which he held captain's rank.

In an address given at Newark, New Jersey, on August 7, 1830, James Shea thus refers to his early years in this country: "Before I could read, I had heard much of the misfortunes of

my own land and much of the glories of yours. I wished to be
an American. At the age of nine, a friend of the family gave
me an American coin bearing the date of my birth. I cherished
it until I arrived at the age of twenty-five, when I emigrated to
your shores, and need I tell you that this little coin reminds me
of my patriotic duty? In New Jersey I first landed, and here
I first met my earliest and best American friend, the later General John A. Schuyler, the liberal, the generous friend of the
exile."

The United States about this time (1829) was entering one
of the most distinctively American periods in its political history.
A new democracy was awake in the country. The westward
movement, with its inevitable reaction upon life in the East, was
in full swing. The building of the canals and the construction
of the highways were levelling old barriers between distant parts
of the land. Industrial conditions were undergoing changes that
amounted in those days to a revolution. Manufacturing was en-
joying a new impetus in the protection the tariff laws afforded; and
in practically every aspect of life, the new era which set in with
Andrew Jackson's accession to the presidency made itself felt
in almost every avenue of human endeavor and achievement,
political and intellectual. To the same causes which had produced these new influences and conditions must also be attributed
the rise of a truly American literature and also a growing interest in the study of American history.

James Shea imparted to his two sons the finer aspects of the
new democracy. They were being reared in a household where
the love of American history dwelt side-by-side with a profound
knowledge of the faith and the history of the Catholic Church.

John Dawson, the younger of the two boys, took naturally to
study. Frail in body and delicate of health, his boyhood was not
marked with the gradual initiation into the games and sports
then prevalent. Rather he took to reading and to the study of
nature. Birds and flowers attracted him especially. Once in
jest, his father called him "Mary," on the score that he was
more like a girl than a boy. The facetious word of a loving
father was not forgotten; and twenty years later, upon entering
the Society of Jesus, John dropped his middle name, Dawson,
and substituted, Gilmary, or Mary's servant, in its stead.

John Dawson Shea received his elementary education in the little academy, in Mulberry Street, near the Cathedral, which the Sisters of Charity of Emmitsburg had opened in 1830. Here he prepared himself for the grammar school connected with Columbia College, where his father was a teacher. In 1833, he passed the entrance examination with success, graduating with honors in 1837, and thus matriculating for Columbia College. But instead of continuing his studies, he entered the counting-house of Señor Don Tomas, a Spanish merchant in the city. It was his duty to meet the ships coming from Spanish ports to New York, to take care of the ship's papers and to assist the Spanish sailors in their purchases. With his unusual aptitude for languages, he quickly acquired a fluent knowledge of Spanish. During the next six years he lost no opportunity for study, his chief interests being botany and history. There is still among his papers, a notebook, entitled "John Dawson Shea's Herbarium for the years 1838, 1839 and, 1840," filled with well-preserved specimens of the rarer flowers that grew in and about New York, and with boyish fancy he has described one of them as a "natural curiosity"—a rose with the bud of another coming out of it, which he found on July 4, 1838. Like most boys who take a lively interest in things that grow, his searches were not confined to flowers, but to all sorts of mineral specimens; and at home his "museum" was soon cluttered up with a variety of finds more precious in his eyes than anything he possessed. It was at this time that he began his valuable collection of coins. Among his papers is a catalogue of the unique coins and medals he sent shortly before his death to the College of Mount Saint Vincent, New York.

To this year (1838) also must be credited his first published essay in the field he was to make so thoroughly his life-work. The *Children's Catholic Magazine,* which had been founded that year, was placed under the versatile direction of Father Felix Varela, who inaugurated a yearly prize, a "handsome gold medal" for "the best original literary article in prose or verse" by any competitor not over the age of eighteen. Young Shea decided to try for the prize and offered an essay on *Cardinal Albornoz.* He did not win the medal, which went to Matthew Horan, of Albany, for his article *A Walk: or a Juvenile Defense of the Catholic*

REV. DR. JOHN POWER, PASTOR OF ST. PETER'S CHURCH, WHO BAPTIZED
JOHN DAWSON SHEA

Religion. Father Varela was so pleased with Shea's essay that he published it in the *Magazine*.

Another eye saw the sign of genius in Shea's paper, that of Bishop John Hughes; and it is significant that at the very time he was preparing to bring the trustee issue to an end, he should praise James Shea's son in the columns of the *Freeman's Journal*.

CHAPTER II

Life's Vocation

(1838-1852)

This encouragement marks a turning point in young Shea's life. During the next few years Shea lost both his father and his mother. Mrs. James Shea died on December 19, 1841, and two years later (December 1, 1843), his father passed away. The two sons were thus left alone in the world. Charles Edward, the elder, was then a member of the bar. About this time John reached his twentieth year; his health had improved so much that he also decided to study law. After two years in a lawyer's office, he stood the examination for entrance into the New York Bar, and was admitted on May 15, 1846. His diploma as solicitor in the State was granted on June 2, 1846.

What his legal practice was for the next two years we do not know, but there is evidence that he had been busily engaged in reading the sources for the colonial history of the Church in this country. The first-fruits of these researches, entitled *Our Martyrs,* appeared in the *United States Catholic Magazine* in 1846-1847, then edited by Rev. Dr. Charles I. White and Rev. Dr. Martin J. Spalding, later Archbishop of Baltimore. These articles, nine in number, attracted attention, and many readers began asking about "J. D. S.," as they were signed. It is probable that Shea contemplated a complete American martyrology. There is a series of articles in the *Ave Maria* (1896-1899), entitled *Martyr Memories of America,* from an unpublished manuscript of Shea's papers. In the volume of the *Magazine* for 1848, Shea published other articles or "notices" on Father Gabriel de la Rebourde, O. F. M., Fathers Du Poisson, Souel, and Senat, S. J., based on sources scarcely known to the Catholic literature of the day.

On March 3, 1846, Shea was elected, upon the nomination of Frederic de Peyster, a resident member of the New York Historical Society, and through association with its members he quickly became known to scholars as one exceptionally familiar with the source-materials for early American history.

The two decades 1830-1850 were remarkable ones in the history of American history writing. Thoughtful scholars whose interest had been aroused by the volumes published by Jared Sparks, Peter Force, George Bancroft, and other writers whom John Spencer Bassett has placed in the middle group of our historians, began to realize that the only true history of our country was that based upon authentic documentary material. Jared Sparks, who had accepted the newly established McLean Chair of History at Harvard in 1838, had considerable influence upon Shea through his published works. It was to Jared Sparks, then president of Harvard University (1849-1853), that John Gilmary Shea dedicated his first historical work: *The Discovery and Exploration of the Mississippi Valley* (New York, 1852).

A second turning-point in Shea's life occurred in 1848, when, as the result of a retreat conducted by Father Michael Driscol, S. J., then of St. John's College, Fordham, the young lawyer decided to ask admission into the Society of Jesus. Fordham had been made the novitiate in 1847, and Shea entered there in July, 1848, signing himself with the name he used ever afterwards, John Gilmary. Father Augustus Thébaud, S. J., was then president of Fordham, and in residence was a galaxy of brilliant and devoted teachers, among whom were Fathers Daubresse, Duranquet, Ryan, Driscol, Pottgeiser, and Schiansky. In the faculty were also Fathers Nash, Ouellet, and Tissot, who were to gain fame as chaplains in the Civil War. In his *History of St. John's College, Fordham,* Taaffe says that Shea was a member of the College faculty in 1848-1849.

In 1850, the novitiate was removed from Fordham to the newly erected St. Mary's College, Montreal, and it is here we find John Gilmary Shea for the next two years. While at Fordham, Shea began his researches for his history of the missions, and during the two years at Montreal, he became the protégé of Father Felix Martin, S. J., the first president of the College, and the acknowledged leader among the Catholic historians of Canada.

Father Martin was born at Auray, in Brittany, on October 4, 1804, and entered the Society of Jesus, in Paris, in 1823. In

1842, he was sent by his superiors to Montreal and in 1850 became president of St. Mary's, which he founded. A decade later (1861) he returned to France, and died in Paris, on November 25, 1892. To Father Martin is due the accumulation of the rich store of documentary material for the study of New France, which he housed in the archives of the College, and it is largely from these materials that John Gilmary Shea was later to draw the precious sources he published in his *Cramoisy Series* from 1857 to 1887. One of Shea's best works is his translation of Father Martin's *Life of Father Jogues,* published in New York in 1885.

To Father Martin's profound influence upon Shea, that of another truly great scholar must be chronicled at this stage of his scholastic development, Edmund Bailey O'Callaghan, the historian of the State of New York. O'Callaghan was older than Father Martin, having been born in Ireland in 1797. No more patient, careful, and judicious investigator of documents has ever delved into American colonial history. Two of O'Callaghan's brothers became priests and were distinguished for their learning. After finishing his studies in Ireland, Edmund Bailey O'Callaghan went to Paris to study medicine. In 1823, he came to Canada, and after finishing his professional studies in Quebec, was admitted to practice in 1827. Later he moved to Montreal, practicing medicine there until the suppression of Papineau's revolt, in which he was seriously involved, led him to seek safety in the United States. Dr. O'Callaghan took up his residence in Albany and there resumed the practice of his profession. "When the anti-rent troubles were attracting attention," Shea wrote in an obituary after his death, "Dr. O'Callaghan began to study the rights of the Patroons, and acquiring a knowledge of Dutch, examined the early Dutch records in the hands of the State and some ancient families." The result of these studies was the publication in 1846 of his *History of New Netherland,* which revealed to American scholars O'Callaghan's outstanding place among the historians of the time.

Dr. O'Callaghan was one of the first to recognize the historical value of the *Jesuit Relations,* and in 1846 read a paper before the New York Historical Society on the subject. Scholars immediately began to try to consult the *Relations,* when this lecture was published (1847), but no complete set was known here or abroad.

It is not certain when Shea, who was twenty-seven years younger than Dr. O'Callaghan, began writing to him; but in the correspondence that remains, the bulk of the letters between 1850 and 1880 are those from the Albany historian. Perhaps, it would be correct to say that Shea, who was always shy and retiring, formed but one real friendship in his life: that with the O'Callaghans, with whom Dr. Shea and Mrs. Shea and the children often exchanged visits in the next quarter of a century. It is evident from the first of the extant letters, dated Albany, July 16, 1850, that correspondence had passed between the two men for several years previous to this time. O'Callaghan writes:

"Your favor of the 26th ulto., postmarked 'Rochester, July 11,' reached me only this morning; and though I should have been made very happy by hearing from you before, I never received the letter you mentioned as having been sent me last year.

"I was still in the belief that you were at Fordham and was consequently much surprised to find you writing from Montreal. However, I was glad to hear of you and from you, as you possess my sincere respect and esteem.

"As you have seen the first Vol. of our *Documentary Hist.* and take such an interest in these matters, and moreover as you are a Citizen of our State, it is only right that you should have the 2nd Vol. I therefore send it to your address, by the express, and hope it will arrive safe, tho' seeing the Postmark of your letter I fear you will have flitted again before this arrives. You will find in the *Papers Relating to Leisler,* some notices of Jesuits in N. Y. and their school on Long Island.

"I thank you for the Notes you send me from the *Roman Catalogue* and would be much obliged if you would allow me to give the extract of that part of your letter in our 3d Vol. now preparing for publication, which will contain a number of Church papers of Colonial times.

"Where could we get a copy of the *Roman Catalogue* mentioned in your letter? I also want a copy of the list of the Canadian Clergy from the earliest time, which is printed in Canada, and a little work by Bishop St. Vallier, entitled *Etat present de l'Eglise et de la Colonie Françoise.* I would willingly pay for these if I could have them, but though I have made divers attempts to procure them, I have not yet succeeded.

"Pray do me the favor to speak to somebody for me in this regard. If they should be left at Mr. Fabre's Book Store for me, he would pay what they should cost & forward them to me.

"It would afford me great pleasure to be able to furnish you copy of Dominie Megapolensis' letter to the Classis of Amsterdam, which one of your Fathers desires.

"You know the Revd. Dr. DeWitt of N. York lent me those Papers. After having made such extracts as I required, I returned the originals and they remain in the Doctor's possession. The letter you refer to was not exclusively on Père Jogues.

"I shall be always glad to hear from you and would esteem it a favour if you could obtain for us a copy of some original Doc. which we could publish in our Vol. of the *Documentary History*.

"P. S. Whenever the French Edition of the *Jesuit Relations* appears, perhaps the Author would please let me have a copy. He will find many errors no doubt in my brochure. But you know under what difficulties it was written.

"Pray have you been admitted to Orders? I fear I do not put the proper address on this letter. If I err, excuse me."

Dr. Shea's historical work for the next forty years was to follow closely the lines O'Callaghan had apparently projected for himself. The letters which passed between the two scholars reveal the fact that the older man, who once playfully addressed Shea as "Brevissime Puer," was an inspiration and a model for America's foremost Catholic historian. In other ways, Edmund Bailey O'Callaghan was able to reach Shea's heart as few of his contemporaries did. Many of the letters have intimate reflections upon the Faith which both men possessed, and there is in the midst of the minute and precious historical data which passed between them the proof of a close and child-like dependence upon the Tabernacle for the support of their health, their families, and their historical studies. As Bishop of Albany (1847-1864), Cardinal McCloskey was Dr. O'Callaghan's firm friend and often called upon him for advice in the temporal affairs of the diocese. Edmund Bailey O'Callaghan died in New York on May 29, 1880, and was buried from St. Patrick's Cathedral, the pall-bearers being Thurlow Weed, John Kelly, George H. Moore, E. F. DeLancey, William S. Preston and John Gilmary Shea.

John Gilmary Shea was at this time (1850), as a scholastic at St. Mary's College, Montreal, Father Martin's assistant in preparing the publication of Father Bressani's *Relation,* which appeared in 1852. Dr. O'Callaghan was then occupied with the publication of the *Documentary History of the State of New York,* and Shea was a medium between him and Father Martin. Many of the notes on Catholic missions and missionaries which Dr. O'Callaghan used came to him in this way. A characteristic letter is one dated Albany, March 11, 1851:

My dear and much esteemed Friend,

"Your obliging favor with the notices of the Early English Catholic Missionaries to these parts was duly received, shortly after its date; and now I have to acknowledge my indebtedness for your esteemed letter of the 2d instant.

"I should have acknowledged your first letter but I postponed it in the hope that I might be able to have sent, ere this, our third Vol. to your address, wherein you would see the use I made of your Memoranda. This Vol. has not yet made its appearance from the Printer, so I shall be deprived for some time longer of the pleasure of sending your copy.

"I am highly gratified to learn that you have been so fortunate as to save those very valuable Mss. to which you refer. In regard to Father Bressani's Work, I hope I may be considered a subscriber for a half a dozen copies. The revd. Father Martin says it is to appear in French and English. Am I to understand that the English copies are to be separate from those in French. Pray let me know this & what the publication price of each copy is to be.

"Now in regard to your proposition for the publication of Extracts from Father Jogues' letter containing a description of New Netherland in 1646 with a sketch of the lives of that Father and Réné Goupil, it is not in my power to give an affirmative answer at present for this reason:——Our publication of another Vol. of the *Doc. History* depends on a vote of the Legislature, which has yet to be passed. Most probably the Legislature will vote it in the course of next month, when I shall be in a position to speak positively.

"Meanwhile if you would have no objection, I would suggest

the propriety of your forwarding me copies of the papers you refer to, that I may submit them to the Secretary of State, under whose supervision the *Documentary History* is prepared. This is a mark of respect due to him. I understand you that they are to be used *as a whole,* and if not used they will be returned to you or to the College as you direct.

"I have to repeat that it is most probable we shall publish a 4th Vol. but we await the order for so doing from the Legislature.

"I read to the Secretary that part of your letter in which you express a wish that your College should obtain a copy of the *Natural History.* This he tells me is within the Jurisdiction of the Regents. If you like, I will make the application for you to Dr. T. Romeyn Beck, Secretary to the Board, on his return to the city from which he is now absent. I do not understand precisely what you mean when you say, 'On the system of M. Vattemare.' His system was exchanging Books for Books. Do you wish it to be understood that the *Natural History* is to be presented to your College in exchange for Books for the State Library? If so, you will have to let me know, and send me a minute of the books you will give in exchange.

"Accompanying this, you will receive a copy of a letter I find here from Père Dablon, Superior of the Jesuit Missions in Canada in 1693. In the *Liste Chronologique* of the Canadian Clergy he is stated (No. 53) as having died 9th Feb. 1680! In the biographical sketch I gave of him, I unfortunately trusted to the authority of this *Liste Chronologique,* and killed the good Priest at least 13 years before his time.

"In the same *Liste* it is stated that Father Simon Lemoine (No. 73) (Jesuit), came to Canada in 1650. Now according to the *Relation* of 1638, p. 75, he was sent in 1638 to the Huron country!

"In like manner, Father Francois Lemercier is put down as arriving in 1650. He came in 1635. (See No. 74).

"Father Paul Ragueneaeu (No. 41) is down as arriving in 1638. He arrived 28th June 1636.

"Thus it is with a number of others, so that in the end the *Liste,* though seemingly published by authority, is worse than useless, for it is the means of leading people astray who confide in it.

"I wish you would be so good as to say to the Revd. Father Martin how much I am obliged to him for the kind trouble he took in investigating the case of that Impostor Williams and his mis-representations. It is a great relief to find that he had no authority for the representation he had made, though when he represented himself as a Clergyman, he almost had shaken the doubt I had first entertained of his statement.

"We are just passing through the Jubilee in this city. This is the last week. During the first week, 1500 of the faithful participated in the Holy Eucharist at St. Mary's (the Bishop's) church, and 2500 at St. John's. The flood of penitents does not seem to be at all diminished. There are two other Catholic Churches here, but the number who have had the benefit of the Holy Father's Indulgence at these, I have no means of ascertaining. I suppose they may be put down at 2000. This however is only one of the two weeks' harvest.

"God has allowed me to be of his flock on this occasion, and I humbly hope with benefit.

"I thank you, dear friend, for your generous recollection of me in your prayers. I hope I may be allowed to think of you at similiar times. I am, indeed, much in need of spiritual aid, for in my life I have experienced many buffetings to which I am still necessarily exposed. *Miserere mei, Deus, secundum magnam misericordiam tuam!*

"Always affectionately yours,"

"E. B. O'CALLAGHAN."

The *Documentary History* opened up to scholars in general and to students of special aspects of American history, like Shea, the wondrous vistas of the Catholic missions which had yet to be explored. The names of Jogues, Brefbeuf, Gabriel Lalemant, Chabanel, Daniel, Garnier, Réné Goupil, and John Lalande— now enrolled since June 21, 1925, in the calendar of the Blessed as the Jesuit Martyrs of North America—and a host of names of other valiant missionaries of the Faith who labored until death that the Name of Christ be made known to the Indians, reawakened as they passed across the pages of Dr. O'Callaghan's volumes the long-forgotten memories of these soldiers of the Cross. The fourth volume (1851) of the *Documentary History* continued the *Description of New Netherland* by Blessed Isaac Jogues, from a copy of the original which was presented by Father Martin to the Regents of the University of New York.

A further influence at work in the critical formation of Shea's historical genius was the *History of the United States* by George Bancroft. Bancroft was the *beau ideal* of the patriotic school of historians who dominated the study of American history from 1829 to 1884. He, too, was Shea's senior by twenty-five years, and had received a far broader training than either O'Callaghan or Shea. The first volume of the *History of the United States from the Discovery of the American Continent,* was published in 1834; the second appeared in 1837; the third in 1840; the fourth and fifth in 1852. These earlier volumes, to use Dr. Jameson's phrase, "voted for Jackson" in their fervid praise of democracy, but they came at a time when the reading of American history was far more popular than it is today, and they captured the public. "The *History* gave Bancroft," Bassett writes, "the undisputed rank of greatest living historian of his country. It made him famous among writers, politicians, and statesmen. No other history written in our country has had the distinction of starting tears in the eyes of an Emerson, opening the doors of high cabinet and diplomatic appointment, and filling its author's pockets with the glittering coin of the republic."

It is probably not generally known that in the earlier editions of his volumes, Bancroft was uniformly fair and generous to the Catholic aspects of American history. But, true to his singular weakness of character, Bancroft yielded to anti-Catholic influences as edition after edition left the press between 1834 and 1883 when the "author's last revision," was published. A comparison between the texts of 1838 and 1883 (Vol. 1, chapter VIII) yields a curious example of the eminent historian's method of weakening or deleting the praise he had given in his original work to Catholic things:

EDMUND BAILEY O'CALLAGHAN

1838	1883
Calvert deserves to be ranked among the most wise and benevolent law-givers of all ages. He was the first in the history of the Christian world to seek for religious security and peace by the practice of justice, and not by the exercise of power; to plan the establishment of popular institutions with the enjoyment of liberty of conscience; to advance the career of civilization by recognizing the rightful equality of all Christian sects. The asylum of Papists was the spot, where in a remote corner of the world, on the banks of rivers which, as yet, had hardly been explored, the mild forbearance of a proprietary adopted religious freedom as the basis of the State.	Sir George Calvert deserves to be ranked among the wisest and most benevolent law-givers for he connected his hopes of the aggrandizement of his family with the establishment of popular institutions; and, being a "Papist," wanted not charity toward Protestants.

This tendency was not visible in the edition Shea was reading, and these volumes stirred his imagination not only with vivid pictures of our colonial history but with the dream of doing something of a similar nature for the Church in the United States.

John Gilmary Shea was not, however, to become an historian of the Bancroft school. His literary ability, like that of O'Callaghan was to be subdued or, at least, to be kept in check by a passionate love of accuracy. Accuracy was not Bancroft's principal gift. He wrote with too much attention to the dramatic effect of his narrative to hesitate over evidence that needed careful establishment before being accepted as historic truth. Basset says of him that the weightiest charge against the *History* is his lack of detachment. He was too strongly partisan by nature to view the past with objective impartiality. "He crystallized all the hero-worship of the old Fourth of July school into a large work written in a style acceptable to the time." But that he awakened a new love of America's past cannot be denied. Sensitively aware of his great success, he was not conscious that the new school of writers growing up about him was preparing itself to look behind his narrative to the sources upon which it was presumably built. Once the new school was properly manned, Bancroft's leadership was at an end.

In this new school John Gilmary Shea can fairly be given the rank of a dauntless pioneer.

Out of his experience as a boy, as a student of law, as a scholastic in one of the foremost educational societies of modern times, as a student under a born inspirer like Father Felix Martin, S. J., he came to the threshold of his historical career, equipped with all those *instruments de travail* which guaranteed the highest scholarship. This zeal was nurtured by the growing friendship with the scholarly Edmund Bailey O'Callaghan. Shea's enthusiasm had been awakened by the glowing pages of Bancroft. Jared Sparks had pointed the way to a more accurate historical knowledge of the past in his collections of the writings of Washington and Franklin. The field before Shea was virgin; for Catholics could point to no historical account of the progress of their Church in the United States. John Gilmary Shea came to the task better qualified than any writer before or since his day.

He belonged to a Society which would have given him conscientiously every available support for the accomplishment of his great ideal—the history of the Catholic Church in the United States. But one drawback was present, and it could not be lightly overcome—his health. Never robust, though never ailing, his friends realized that only the greatest care would carry him to mature manhood. It was this drawback, in fact, which was to bring in 1852 a third and final turning-point to his future.

The last year of his stay in Canada was filled with preoccupation about his vocation. There is very little in his papers to tell us of the struggle he underwent, although a commonplace book, filled with Latin and French quotations from spiritual writers on the necessity of placing full confidence in God, with here and there a prayer for light in his difficulty, gives proof that the decision he was to make in 1852 was not easily reached. In the faintest ink, but still visible owing to his perfect penmanship, is a note in this book which reads: "June 5, 1851—Visited the tomb of Catherine Tegakwitha and promised to build a stone cross there if my prayer was granted—my novena ended." This excursion to the burial place of the Lily of the Mohawks, at Caughnawaga, Canada, marks the beginning of the decision he took before the end of that year.

Late in 1851, he asked permission to return to Fordham. There is a letter in the archives of the New York Historical Society, dated January 3, 1852, from Rev. John Gilmary Shea, S. J., addressed to George H. Moore, its Secretary, giving an account of some investigations Shea had made in the history of the Jesuit missions in colonial New England and New York. Another letter (April 6, 1852) in the same archives, shows that on that date he presented to the Historical Society the original map of Father Marquette's discovery and exploration of the Mississippi in the year 1673. These two items are interesting, since it is upon these subjects his first two volumes, published within the next two years, were to be based.

To Edmund Bailey O'Callaghan, he wrote from St. Francis Xavier College, New York, on April 29, 1852, "Excuse me, if I have not written before this and write now only a hasty line: but in truth I have been so harrassed and unsettled that for months past and even now I do not know where or what I am. I can hardly give any definite address, yet anything addressed here will reach me. I had hoped to see you ere this, but such has not been the case. When may I hope it? My principal object in writing now is to ask you to send me Fr. Jogues' account of Goupil's death. Let me know too when the 4th vol. will be out as I do not wish the Hist. Society to take the lead of you."

By June, 1852, Shea had made up his mind fully about his vocation for the priesthood, and had decided to leave the Society of Jesus. He announced the fact to Dr. O'Callaghan, who wrote to him from Albany, on June 19, of that year: "The information you communicate has excited my most lively sympathy. But I am encouraged to hope that all will yet turn out well by you giving me to understand that you only pause in order to reflect.

I like the man that runs and rallies: was the observation of Frederick the Great. Others like you, weary of study, nerves unstrung and temper chafed, are apt to bolt for a while. I had a brother who came home from Maynooth, desponding and hopeless, who yet rallied, went to the Irish College at Paris, volunteered for the West Indies Mission to labor among the Blacks and laid down his life at St. Lucia for the honor and glory of God. He who takes up the Cross to follow Him Who died on it, must be prepared to feel the burthen and the heat of the day, and be ready, too, to bear it. May God direct you, my young friend, is my earnest and sincere prayer."

Although he left the Society of Jesus definitely that summer, this was not the last letter he received, addressed to Rev. John Gilmary Shea, S. J. There is a small book among his papers, containing hundreds of envelopes covering the next thirty years, and a goodly portion of them are addressed to "Rev. John Gilmary Shea, S. J." It is curious to find him called Rev. John Gilmary Shea in a Source Book for American Church History, published as late as 1921. In fact forty-seven years after his departure from Fordham, at the time of his accident in 1889, a leading New York newspaper carried the notice: "Rev. Dr. Shea has a bad fall." Almost up to his death, his foreign correspondents insisted on addressing him as Reverend, and as late as 1886, Catholic priests in various sections of the country, writing to him for information or for copies of his historical works, use the same title.

CHAPTER III

(1852-1857)

When John Gilmary Shea made his first appearance in public
(December 9, 1852) to read a paper on the *Early Catholic Missions of the United States,* before the Catholic Institute of New
York City, little had been accomplished either for the preservation of historical material relating to the Church in this country
or for the study of Catholic missionary effort in spreading the
Gospel in the New World.

These materials were rapidly perishing. Much had been
wantonly, or ignorantly, destroyed, and Shea realized that only
by awakening the consciousness of the entire Catholic public in
the United States could the hand of the destroyers, Catholic and
non-Catholic, be stopped. For forty years (1852-1892) he made
this the object of his life's work.

In one of his editorials in the *Catholic News* (June 5, 1891),
he wrote:

"Every year in the houses and institutions of Catholics more
historical material is destroyed than five historical societies will
hereafter be able to collect in twenty years. For the early Spanish and French period and part of the country much was printed,
but the great archives of New Mexico have been wantonly destroyed in our time by Federal officials, ignorant or venal
interlopers from abroad, who knew nothing and cared nothing
for the early history of the Catholic territory. In our time much
of the archives of the California missions has been scattered,
and fragments are used by our enemies to make the Catholic
Church and its work ridiculous in the eyes of the public. The
records of our oldest churches are neglected, and are gradually
disappearing. Even our printed material is difficult to reach.
There is scarcely one perfect set of the *Catholic Directories.* We
have never seen a perfect set of any of the older Catholic newspapers. The collection of the earliest Catholic books printed in
this country which the Rev. J. M. Finotti formed at great expense

and labor was scattered to the winds, no Catholic making an
effort to preserve it intact. Letters of early Catholic missionaries
or of Catholic laymen who were zealous for the faith are constantly destroyed.

"Here is work for Catholic Historical Societies, and an immense work requiring patience, faith, perseverance and a spirit
of sacrifice. It behooves us to act or to be disgraced. Those who
come after us will not spare us in their just and sweeping con-
demnation if the present apathy continues. Non-Catholic
institutions and libraries are waking up to the importance of
collecting the once despised Catholic material. When in an auc-
tion room a rare Catholic book or pamphlet turns up, the
Catholic who wishes to buy finds that his competitors are not
Catholics or very rarely so."

To bring home to his Catholic fellow-citizens first of all, and
then to their non-Catholic neighbors, the claims of the Church in
the discovery, the civilization, and the building of the nation, he
labored day and night in the midst of difficulties that might have
stemmed the enthusiasm of any one except a genius like himself.

Years afterwards, at the close of his life he wrote (April 20,
1891) to Monsignor Loughlin, of Philadelphia, that he had discovered a host of facts relating to the negligence of those in
authority towards the archival sources for American Catholic
history. "Not only has little been done," he wrote, "but some
of that little has been destroyed. A Father Ulrich, one of the
early Benedictines of St. Vincent's Abbey, kept a diary for
many years, so that the volumes formed a pile several feet high,
recording every event in the community and in the Church in
that part of western Pennsylvania. They were all destroyed by
order of Abbot Wimmer. Bishop de St. Palais ordered all the
papers of the Vincennes diocese, gathered, bound and indexed
by his predecessor, to be destroyed. These were cases of delib-
erate destruction, while of those resulting from ignorance and
indifference it would be impossible to make a record. The Archbishop of New York has really no archives; no papers of Bishops
Connolly or Dubois; Archbishops Hughes and McCloskey. The
relatives of Archbishop Hughes, I find, destroyed all his letters.
The papers of the Reverend John Power, V. G., and twice
Administrator of New York, were placed in a religious house

for preservation. In time they were in the way and were destroyed. It is greatly to be regretted that priests do not write, at least, the edifying and interesting events in their ministry. There are few priests who could not relate many, but alas they are seldom recorded. Unless you object I shall use your letter in an article and thus hope to draw attention to the matter. *We may influence some one in authority."*

Almost on the threshold of the grave, a fortnight before his death in 1892, he felt obliged to publish a stern challenge to Catholics not to stand aside in that centenary year of the discovery of America and to allow those not of the Faith to assume all the glory of America's past. In a passage that should be known to every American Catholic boy and girl in our schools, he says: "Who discovered and colonized Greenland and had cathedral church and convent there? Catholics. If Vinland was really part of this country, who discovered and visited it. Lief Ericson, a Catholic, with his Catholic Northmen, followed by Catholic bishops and priests. As to Christopher Columbus and his Catholicity there is no question. Who explored the Atlantic and Gulf Coast of the United States? Catholic Navigators: John and Sebastian Cabot; John Ponce de Leon; Pineda, first to see the Mississippi and name it the River of the Holy Ghost; Miruelo; Verrazzano; Gomez; Cordillo; and Ayllon—all Catholics. Who explored the Mississippi from its northern waters to the Gulf of Mexico? The Catholic Franciscan, Hennepin, and Du Lhut, a Catholic; Joliet, a Catholic; Father Marquette, a Jesuit; LaSalle and his Franciscan chaplains, Catholics; DeSoto, Tristan de Luna, and other Spanish explorers, all Catholics. Who discovered and named the St. Lawrence? Cartier, a Catholic. Who made it known to the Upper Lake? Champlain, a Catholic, the first to map its course. The *Jesuit Relations* first gave the maps of Lake Ontario and Lake Superior. The Sulpitian Dollier de Casson drew the first map of Lake Erie. Fathers Jogues and Raymbaut planted the cross at Sault Ste. Marie. A Jesuit discovered the salt springs of Onondaga; a Franciscan, the oil springs near Lake Erie; Catholic Missionaries first described Niagara. The Catholic De la Verendrye first reached the Rocky Mountains; Menendez, a Catholic, and Oñate, a Catholic, founded our two oldest cities, Saint Augustine and

Santa Fé, which in their very names tell of their Catholic origin. Who first studied the languages of our Indian tribes and reduced them to grammatical forms so as to use them in bringing the heathen natives to a knowledge of God and Christ the Redeemer? Catholic missionaries. Rale, in Maine; Bruyas, Garnier and other Jesuits, in New York; White, in Maryland; Paraja, in Florida; Le Boullenger, in Illinois; Arroyo de la Guesta and other Franciscans, in California; Serra, Garcia and their companions, in Texas; and at a late day, Baraga, Marcoux, Becourt, Mengarini, Gailland, Vetromile, Giorda, Palladino. In this anniversary year who can wipe these glorious names from the obelisk of fame"?

If John Gilmary Shea could write in all justness on the occasion of receiving the first Laetare Medal in 1883, "What I have done is little, terribly little, in comparison to the work that lies untouched," it can be conceded without argument that when he began his historical activities in 1852, practically nothing worthy of the great Church had been written. The Catholic newspapers had, it is true, kept alive in a fitful way an interest in the historical past of their localities. Serious literary reviews—such as the *Metropolitan* which lasted a year (Baltimore, 1830); the *Religious Cabinet,* which also lasted a year (Baltimore, 1842); and the *United States Catholic Magazine,* which was published for six years (Baltimore, 1842-1848) under the skilled editorship of Dr. Charles I. White; and the *Catholic Expositor,* edited by Felix Varela, D. D. and Charles Constantine Pise, D. D., in New York City, from 1841 to 1846, were published monthly and not only gave a literary medium for Catholic scholarship, but incidentally preserved much historical material which otherwise would have been lost. Bernard H. Campbell's *Memoirs of the Life and Times of the Most Rev. John Carroll, first Archbishop of Baltimore,* which appeared in the *United States Catholic Magazine* from 1844 to 1848, was the first noteworthy attempt to gather up the historical fragments that remained, and a comparison between his studies and the little biography of the Father of the American hierarchy, published by Robert Brent in Baltimore in 1843, shows how inadequate the latter volume was. One by one, these monthly periodicals were obliged to cease publication. In offering the seventh volume (1848) of the *United States*

Catholic Magazine to the public, Dr. Charles I. White regretted "to be under the necessity of stating that the patronage extended to the work does not justify him in continuing its publication. It has been issued for some time with a loss to the proprietor, and he cannot consent to make any further sacrifices for the purpose of sustaining it." Orestes A. Brownson had resumed the publication of his *Review* in January, 1844, and after his reception into the Church in October of that year, *Brownson's Quarterly Review* quickly became one of the foremost Catholic apologetical magazines in the English language. But Brownson was essentially a philosopher and theologian, and it was his defence of the Faith in these fields which won him the public approbation of the last of the national Provincial Councils, held in Baltimore in 1849. Historical articles of eminent value were never absent from its pages, but they were of a general nature, sometimes so recondite that they chilled writers who aspired to see their essays appear in so formidable a literary magazine. When the *Metropolitan* was resurrected as a monthly magazine in 1853, it was devoted more "to Religion, Education, Literature and General Information" than to historical subjects; although many valuable papers on American Catholic history were printed in its pages during the six years it existed (1853-1859).

In the second volume of the *Metropolitan* (July, 1854), there is an article by John Gilmary Shea, entitled *Catholic Literature in the United States*. He chronicles the work done in the fields of theology, literature, and history, up to that time. Among the historians of merit, he lists Father Felix Martin, S. J., Edmund Bailey O'Callaghan, Father William McSherry, S. J., Dr. Pise, Martin J. Spalding, Dr. Charles I. White, Archbishop Bayley, Bernard U. Campbell, and Xavier D. Macleod.

Before the appearance of Shea's *Discovery and Exploration of the Mississippi Valley,* in 1852, the historiographer has very little of value to chronicle in the field of American Catholic history. The *Discovery and Exploration* does not make a dividing line in American Catholic historiography; it is in reality the beginning of activity in this special field of American scholarship. The work won an immediate success. The arrangement of the book was similar to that of O'Callaghan's *Documentary History.* In fact, some of the most valuable material which went

into the *Discovery and Exploration* had been offered by Shea to
the State of New York for inclusion in O'Callaghan's volumes,
but was not accepted. For a time Dr. Shea was under the impression that O'Callaghan was responsible for the rejection of
his manuscripts and the incident caused a temporary rift in their
friendship.

On receipt of the *Discovery and Exploration,* O'Callaghan
wrote to him (November 18, 1852) : *"Quid retribuam tibi, caris-
sime amice, pro libro tuo elegantissimo?* I was looking for it
with great desire, having had my appetite whetted by a notice in
the *Literary World.* Marquette and LaSalle, and above all, the
Great West, owe you very much. And I sincerely trust you will
reap a proper reward for your patient and valuable labors." The
leading reviews of England and America welcomed Shea's first
volume as one of the most noteworthy contributions to American
history in recent years. All who perused the volume recognized
that here was a scholar who would go far in his chosen vocation
The contents of the book was made up of documents not accessible to scholars, and the critical notes appended to his pages
revealed an uncommon knowledge of colonial history. The unusual elegance of the printing and the binding found favor
in the eyes of collectors, and the edition was exhausted before
the end of the year. The volume was not only one of picturesque
interest, but of profound original research; and not the least of
the surprises it contained was the original map of the Marquette-
Joliet expedition of 1673, in Marquette's own handwriting.

The *Discovery and Exploration* contained the original narrative of Marquette, Membré, Hennepin, and Anasase Douay,
together with the *Relation* of Dablon and several unpublished
documents relating to La Salle. The *Westminster Review* called
it "a most valuable and interesting volume," and the London
Athenaeum says: "Mr. Shea writes clearly, graphically, and with
considerable eloquence." Apart from the critical notes in the
volume, Shea's contribution consists of a *Bibliographical Notice
of Father Louis Hennepin,* a *History of the Discovery of the
Mississippi River,* a *Life of Father Marquette,* and a notice of
Sieur Joliet.

Shea's renaissance of interest in these narratives met a first
caustic rebuff from Dr. Brownson who with his old colonial

prejudice against the French of Canada, ridiculed in his *Review* for October, 1853, the value of these sources for accurate history. "None of them," he wrote, "unless we except Charlevoix, is worthy to be called a history." He then adds a sentence which struck Shea as being deliberately insulting: "None which a Canadian could peruse without blushing for the patience which allowed ignorance or prejudice thus to confound the whole interests of a people with the toils of a poor missionary among the savages or the experience of an attaché of the government."

Dr. Shea answered Brownson in a remarkably eloquent paper published in the *Metropolitan* for March and April, 1855. "For ourselves," Shea writes, "Who have been for years reading the sources of Canadian history and found such sources to be almost exclusively the work of missionaries, we are grieved and pained at such a charge. We cannot conceive how any Canadian could blush to read Bressani's work, the *Relation* of 1649, that of 1644, the narrative of Marquette, or the work of Sagard. On the contrary, we think that the Canadian, or the man, even of the most Rome-hating sect, that can read these without emotion, must be devoid of every noble feeling; and if a Canadian, as destitute of all patriotism as Benedict Arnold. If Dr. Brownson ever read these works, he certainly never could have penned so gross a charge."

Shea's article *Canada and her Historians* is another stage in his advance, for in replying to Brownson's apparent ignorance of the sources, he notes a series of volumes and reprints which American historians needed for colonial history. All of these, even including the great task of giving us the first complete translation of Charlevoix's *History and General Description of New France,* he was able to accomplish before his death.

The *Discovery and Exploration* had an appeal for the scholar and collector. Shea's next volume *History of the Catholic Missions among the Indian Tribes of the United States, 1529-1859,* published by the New York publishing firm he had entered, the Dunigans, brought the story of missionary effort by the Spanish, French, and English priests to every Catholic fireside. Here was a volume which all could read and understand. It was the result of ten years' collection of materials and historical research. The idea of the work grew out of the lecture he had given in

1852 before the Catholic Institute, though the actual incentive came from Jared Sparks, then president of Harvard University.

Shea's labor on this volume must have been enormous, for the sources he quotes and uses make up a creditable library of early Americana. Even Brownson, who was apt to disparage any glory given to the French Catholic missionaries, confessed that the book was "a work of solid merit, entitling the author to an honorable rank among our historical writers."

The *History of the Catholic Missions* was the most valuable volume that had been issued from the American Catholic press up to that time; and edition followed edition in rapid succession until the Civil War. Other writers, especially Bancroft, Sparks, O'Callaghan, Kip and others, had not stinted their praise in dealing with the Catholic missionaries and had given them a merited place in the country's history. But what Shea wished to do was to show that the result of their labors was a permanent one and that to deny them any lasting success was an unfair use of historical criticism. "The great decrease of the Indians," Shea says, "may indeed in part excuse some writers from not knowing the real state of little communities, now hemmed in by the busy whites; and it would excuse them, were it not very evident that they decide the results of the missions, not from observation, but from preconceived ideas of the Catholic Church. One remarkable fact will, at all events, appear in the course of this work, that the tribes evangelized by the French and Spaniards subsist to this day, except where brought in contact with the colonists of England and their allies or descendants; while it is notorious that the tribes in the territory colonized by England, have in many cases entirely disappeared, and perished without ever having had the gospel preached to them. The Abnakis, Caughnawagas, Kaskaskias, Miamis, Ottawas, Chippeways, Arkansas, and the New Mexican tribes remain, and number faithful Christians; but where are the Pequods, Narragansetts, the Mohegans, the Mattowax, the Lenape, the Powatans? They live only in name in the rivers and mountains of our land."

Dr. Shea for the first time gives us a glimpse in the preface of his volume, to his historical spirit. "In writing," he says, "I have endeavored to be just to all men, to avoid all partiality, to take no part in the rivalries which have existed and still exist, all tending to overshadow the truth, and give theories or party views for a real picture of the historical facts."

There was a charm and an eloquence about the *History of the Catholic Missions* which attracted all who read his dramatic description of what Catholic priests had undergone to plant the seeds of the Faith in the New World. Shea's volume did more than tell the story of that past. It brought out in clear relief the legacy the missionaries of old had bequeathed to the generation of Catholics for whom he was writing; and in more than one place, high and low, his pages awakened the pertinent question: what was the Catholic Church of the United States doing to preserve the Faith among the Catholic Indian tribes which had survived the white man's onward advance towards the West?

Honors of a kind that have an intimate pleasure to the historian began to come to him. We find, from 1855 onwards, the Historical Societies of the country electing him to resident, corresponding and honorary membership. The earliest among these honors came in February 1854, from the State Historical Society of Wisconsin. The Massachusetts Historical Society and the Maryland Historical Society brought him into their ranks in 1855. There was, indeed, no longer any doubt where John Gilmary Shea stood in the esteem of his co-laborers in American history.

Dr. Shea was at this time thirty years old. Although he had resumed the practice of law in New York after leaving the Society of Jesus in 1852, his tastes lay more in the field of research; and when the success of the *Missions* encouraged him to believe that in history lay his true vocation, he lost no time in planning his future life.

During these two years he was a frequent guest in social circles and he was a familiar figure at meetings where the cause of Irish freedom was discussed. It was at this time he met and courted Miss Sophie Savage. They were married by Rev. Dr. Cummings in the summer of 1854. Miss Savage was the daughter of John and Julia (Barrenger) Savage, and was related to several prominent Puritan families of New England, among them the Penfields and the Brainerds, to the latter of which belonged the well-known Indian missionary, Rev. David Brainerd. The marriage proved to be a very happy one in every respect.

Mrs. Shea was unfailing in her co-operation during the forty years of their life together, and their two daughters, Ida and Emma Isabel, the latter of whom is still living, were trained by her to be competent aids to their father in his numerous and complex activities.

In one of O'Callaghan's letters, dated September 28, 1854, we have an amusing message to Shea after his marriage: "My wife and I received a very suspicious sort of missive from you in the forepart of the summer, indicating that you were about to cast off, and abandon, the single state of blessedness. We deferred acknowledging its receipt until we should have the pleasure to do so in person, on our pilgrimage to the seaside. And when the time came, we were lured Northward, even unto the Saratoga Springs, where we sojourned until the close of the season. We have not, therefore, been your way: we hope to go down before New Year's. If we do, we'll present ourselves in due form. Meanwhile, we try to tender, though late, our sincere felicitations, and hope you wear your chains, like the Greek slave, gracefully. You will anticipate my intentions, I hope, and introduce me, on receipt hereof, proxy-cally, to your *cara sposa.* Keep my imperfections in the background, and paint me as you wish your friend to be, not as he is. I'll endeavor to come up to your mark, if you only let me know how high it is."

Unlike his first volume, Shea's *History of the Catholic Missions* appealed to Catholics in every part of the country, and soon letters began to come in great numbers to the Shea household asking for information, advice and guidance in the historical studies his work had aroused. Out of this correspondence one fact may be chosen because around it centres a curious and regrettable incident in American Catholic research.

The future Archbishop Bailey, than Secretary to Archbishop Hughes, published in 1853 his valuable little *Sketch of the History of the Catholic Church on the Island of New York,* based upon sources found in B. U. Campbell's articles, in the publications of O'Callaghan, and in a host of manuscripts, many of which had been furnished to him by Dr. Shea. Among the documents in Dr. Bayley's possession at the time were the private letters and papers of Bishop Bruté of Vincennes. Dr. Bruté's life as a priest and bishop in this country (1810-1839) coincided with some of the most important years in Catholic American history. His life in France (1779-1810) was a remarkable one, and his notes and reminiscences of scenes connected with the French Revolution were unique. It was Bishop Bruté's custom to keep a Note Book into which he entered daily matters of importance, often accompanying them with sketches of events as he saw them. He carried on an extensive correspondence with the leading American Catholic prelates and laymen of the day (1810-1839) and wrote considerably to foreign correspondents. Bishop Bruté seems to have realized the value of his manuscript materials, for there are several outlines and plans from his pen in the Baltimore Cathedral Archives for a *History of the Church in America.*

It is said that he spent the last months of his life in putting all these historical papers into order for his literary executor. These extensive archives were bequeathed to his successor, Bishop de la Hailandière. When the latter resigned the See of Vincennes, and set out for France, he prevailed upon Archbishop Hughes, who had known Simon Gabriel Bruté intimately at Mount St. Mary's, Emmitsburg, to undertake a *Life of Bishop Bruté.* Dr. Hughes accepted the task, and de la Hailandière gave orders to the priest in charge of the Cathedral at Vincennes to forward the entire collection to New York.

Archbishop Hughes found it impossible to secure the leisure necessary for the task, and when Dr. Bayley's *Sketch* appeared, it was hoped that the young priest would take up the long-deferred project of Bruté's *Life.* On several occasions the officials of the Vincennes Diocese had endeavored to have the Bruté Mss. returned to their archives, but without success. A letter from Dr. James A. Causten, of Washington, D. C., to Father Bayley, regarding the papers, brought the following answer, in which it will be seen, the generally accepted tradition that the New York ecclesiastical authorities were responsible for their loss, cannot be sustained. Father Bayley writes (June 9, 1852):

"The Papers of the late B'p Bruté were far from being complete when they came into the Archbishop's hands; they had evidently been examined by some one, who had taken from them many important papers, especially of an historical nature. When they first arrived here, I examined them myself, in the hope of

finding important information upon certain matters, to which
I had turned my attention—and discovered nothing worth preserving, though during his whole life he had employed more or
less time in making researches connected with the history of the
Catholic Religion in this part of the world. As however I did
not examine them particularly in reference to the Indian Missions, there may be some documents connected with them, that
I may have overlooked—and I will take an early opportunity of
looking them over again so that if I discover anything likely
to interest you, I will let you know. The Rev. Mr. Shea of the
Society of Jesus, has been for some time engaged upon a History
of the Jesuit Missions amongst the Indians—and from his pecu-
liar fitness for the task, as well as the valuable documents in his
possession, I have no doubt that it will prove a valuable addition
to the early history of our country."

What had happened to the Bruté papers will probably never
be known. Father Audran of Vincennes made an attempt to
have them sent back, but Bishop Bayley refused to give them
up. That Shea was also refused access to the collection is certain from his letter to Father Audran, dated November 20, 1854:
"Bishop Bayley told me that he had Bishop Bruté's letters and
papers. I did not however get access to them. Though I hinted
my wish very clearly, I forebore to press it as I thought that,
though once intended for the Church, my actual lay position
would be an obstacle to my rummaging a Bishop's papers . . . .
I deemed it careless to allow such a mass of documents to be
exposed to perish and wondered at it. The whole may be reme-
died by a letter from Msgr. de St. Palais to Bishop Bayley, asking the return of the Bruté manuscripts; and once returned, I
would urge their being bound in volumes and indexed to be preserved as diocesan archives . . . . This will not only facilitate
reference but will prevent abstraction."

The first to profit by Shea's success as a writer was the firm
of Dunigan and Brother with which he was connected. In
quick succession Shea edited for this publishing house a *General
History of Modern Europe* (1854), a book of 485 pages in duodecimo; and a *First Book of History, combined with Geography
and Chronology for younger Classes* (1854, 12 mo., pp. 254).
which Brownson noticed favorably in his *Review* (Jan. 1855).

An *Elementary History of the United States* (pp. 157) was writen for the Sadliers and published in 1855; and that same year he published a *Catechism of the History of the United States* (pp. 180). The house of Dunigan published (1857) his *School History of the United States from the Earliest Period to the Present Time* (pp. 288). These works have not survived as text books, though they were popular in their day. They are to be regarded rather as outward signs of the pressure Dr. Shea experienced during these years in providing for his growing family.

Strange as it may seem, although he was the pioneer in the field, John Gilmary Shea was not to be the first writer to treat the general history of the Catholic Church in the United States.

In 1855, Thomas D'Arcy McGee published at Boston his *Catholic History of North America* in five parts, to which he appended several *Documents illustrative of the Catholic History of America.* McGee's little volume (pp. 239) is written in his best journalistic style and was immensely popular with Catholic readers during the later part of the Know-Nothing movement. The sources used are mainly O'Callaghan's *Documentary History,* Shea's *Discovery and Exploration,* Kip's *Jesuits in America,* Bishop Bayley's *Sketch,* Spalding's *Life of Flaget,* Brent's *Carroll* and the current popular histories of the United States. Shea's *Catholic Missions* was not used. A note on page 63 of McGee's book says: "After the above was written we learned with sincere pleasure that Mr. John Gilmary Shea had a work in the press in which the American missions will be treated of very fully." Nearly fifty pages of the Appendix are devoted to Catherine Tegakwitha. McGee's work must be considered, therefore, as the initial attempt during the first sixty-five years of the organized hierarchy in this country to write a connected history of the Church in the United States.

It is no disparagement to Dr. Shea's greater works to say that his *History of the Catholic Missions among the Indian Tribes* is the best organized of all his writings. The divisions of the book are natural. Source-references to manuscript material and to books then unknown to the greater part of historical writers abound in the volume; and the whole book has the appearance of a well-conceived plan, thoroughly worked out. It is to be regretted that Dr. Shea did not so plan his next volume

The Catholic Church in the United States: a Sketch of its Ecclesiastical History, which he published in co-authorship with Henry DeCourcy, in 1856.

There are many questions one would like to have answered about this volume. The original edition carried a dedicatory letter in French "A son Excellence Monsigneur Cajetan Bedini, Archévêque de Thebes, Nonce Apostolique, etc.," dated New York, May 3, 1856, and signed by Dr. Shea, although it is written in the first person by DeCourcy. This same edition carried as an appendix some thirty pages of documents relating to Bedini's visit to the United States in 1853-1854.

Upon his appointment as Nuncio to the Court of Brazil in 1853, Archbishop Bedini was instructed to proceed to Washington and to present to President Pierce a friendly letter from the Holy See. He reached New York on June 30, 1853, and after presenting his diplomatic credentials began a tour of the country for the purpose of studying certain conditions which had been brought to the attention of Piux IX. An apostate Italian priest, Gavazzi, began spreading vile calumnies against the Nuncio, and these soon found their way into the public press and aroused fanatical demonstrations in several cities which Bedini visited. In Cincinnati an armed attempt was made by a group of Germans to sack the house in which he was residing. Anti-Catholic German societies in several places threatened the Nuncio's life, and it is deplorable that, at a time when we had a Chargé d'Affaires at the Papal Court in Rome, the Government of the United States took no measures to protect the envoy of the Holy See. Before leaving New York to return to Rome, Archbishop Bedini had engraved in that city copies of the Madonna of Rimini as a gift to his many friends. The inscription bore the words "edified and grateful"—edified by all he had seen of Catholic progress in the United States and grateful for the reception he had everywhere received from the faithful. Archbishop Bedini's conduct was flawless, bordering indeed on the heroic. He went about from city to city as if the demonstrations against him were too negligible to notice, and once he took up his residence in any city, he proceeded to keep all the engagements he had made— dedicating churches, ordaining priests, opening ecclesiastical retreats, presiding at college commencements, visiting hospitals and

MATER MISERICORDIAE.

MGR. BEDINI'S SOUVENIR OF HIS VISIT

orphanages—with an incomparable dignity which won for him the admiration of non-Catholics everywhere.

Some time after Bedini's departure, Henry de Courcy de la Roche Heron, then a merchant in New York, who spent his leisure time in contributing sketches of the Church here to the *Ami de la Religion,* the *Univers,* and other Catholic periodicals in France, publicly (April 8, 1854) undertook to answer the charges made against the illustrious visitor. After considerable correspondence with authorities in Bologna and Rome, De Courcy succeeded in obtaining all the necessary documents for his purpose. Archbishop Hughes dissuaded him from publishing the documents at the time, owing to the continuance of popular feeling against Bedini through Know-Nothing channels, and De Courcy, who then engaged Dr. Shea's collaboration for his *Essais sur l'Histoire de la Religion Catholique des Etats-Unis,* decided to wait until Dr. Shea had completed the translation of his essays for the volume they both had in mind.

This will explain the following passage from the French preface: "En quittant les Etas-Unis, Votre Excellence nous laissait un pieux souvenir de sa munificence et de sa devotion en se declarant *edifié et reconnaissant.* C'est bien plutôt aux Catholiques des Etas-Unis de se proclamer *edifiés* de vos vertus et *reconnaissants* de vos bienfaits; et l'hommage que je vous presente, en commun avec le savant écrivain, Mr. John G. Shea, qui s'est complaisamment associé a mon travail, est un faible tribut de (est un faible tribut) de notre mutuelle gratitude, et de notre complet dévouement au Saint Siège Apostolique."

Dr. Shea aided De Courcy with all the manuscript materials, books and pamphlets he had collected, and consented to prepare a translation of the essays for the American public, owing, as he says, to "the want of any regular history of the Catholic Church in the United States."

After the translation was completed, Dr. Shea went over the whole volume adding paragraphs here and there, supplying references, and in some cases writing new chapters for the book. "From the close friendship which united us," he says, "and from our daily intercourse during the progress of the work, it would be difficult now for me to state what portions are exclusively mine." The truth is that Shea's characteristic modesty prevented

him from claiming the entire work as his own. He had guided
the articles in French as they were written by De Courcy, had
then translated them into English, and then rewritten the whole
from further sources at his disposal.

The *Catholic Church in the United States,* which came practically to be called the De Courcy-Shea *History,* purported to be
a general history of the Church in this country. As such it remained but a torso until 1879, when Shea published a revised
edition, not only filling in the many gaps of the edition of 1856,
but bringing the narrative down to date. The original volume
covers but three of the five dioceses created in 1808: Baltimore,
Philadelphia, and New York. Boston is not mentioned; Bards-
town and the other dioceses erected between 1808 and 1853 are
ignored. The volume which contains almost six hundred pages,
did not meet with the same welcome as the *History of the Catholic Missions.* Brownson was especially savage in his criticism of
the book, calling it "a series of newspaper articles, if we may
so speak, on Church matters in the United States, hastily thrown
off and carelessly strung together." And yet, critics sought in
vain for serious inaccuracies in the work. When the revised
and enlarged edition appeared in 1879, Dr. Shea could write in
all justice: "The present work, in its original form, relating
mainly to the origin and early progress of the Church in this
country, has been for many years the only work affording the
reader any general view of the advancement of our holy Faith.
It has been referred to as authority on numberless occasions, and
its general accuracy admitted by all." Again, in 1892, in the
preface to his greatest work, Dr. Shea says that the De Courcy-
Shea volume "has been for some thirty years the most compre-
hensive account accessible of the history of the Church in this
country."

Limited as it is in point of time, the DeCourcy-Shea *History*
is a veritable treasure-trove for the research student. Not only
in the wide range of the sources it mentions, but in the variety
of information which cannot be obtained elsewhere, the book
is indispensible to all writers in the field. That many of the
harsh criticisms in the Catholic press levelled against the volume
were unjust can now be admitted. To one of these criticisms,

which appeared in the Boston *Pilot,* Dr. Shea replied in the columns of that paper on March 10, 1860:

"Within the last two months I have noticed two flings at De Courcy's *Catholic Church* in your columns. One spoke of the 'De Courcy blunders,' another says that the *Catholic Almanac* without circularizing each clergyman will be of no more use to the future historian of Catholicity in the U. S. than De Courcy's histories.

"My acquaintance with Mr. De Courcy began with his calling upon me for information, and I then put at his hisposal all my collection and the knowledge which several years' attention to the subject afforded me. After he wrote his sketches, I corrected what I found erroneous, and three Bishops, with several clergymen, revised them carefully, and made still more corrections.

"Now there are still errors, there are omissions, important omissions even, that I have since discovered, and can correct. The mass of the book is, however, strictly correct, and to treat it as a book utterly unreliable, is a position that is easily taken, but not so easily justified. I think it most unfair, uncourteous and un-Catholic.

"As I closed in 1859 my fifteen years' labor as a Catholic writer, never again probably to appear in that character, I have no personal interest or feeling in the matter, but I solicit as an act of merest justice, between man and man, that the Catholic historical students of the country, many of whom doubtless have devoted far more talent, means and industry to the reasearch and to the collection of materials than I have, will not content themselves with talking of blunders, but send a full, distinct note of them to some Catholic paper, or, if they deem it more in accordance with Christian charity, to the Translator and Editor of De Courcy's *Catholic Church,* John Gilmary Shea."

Henry De Courcy died in France in 1862, and Dr. Shea was obliged to bear the brunt of the attacks on the book, almost up to the publication of the first volume of his own *History* in 1886. Among the few who never failed to pick flaws in Shea's historical work was Martin I. J. Griffin, of Philadelphia. In answer to one of Griffin's articles on the volume, Dr. Shea wrote as follows (Elizabeth, N. J., March 3, 1883):

"I have read the article you enclosed and must say frankly that I think it extremely dishonest. There is not a particle of proof that De Courcy was a romancer.

"Watson's *Annals* had been in the hands of Catholic and Protestant for years. Its statements about the old Priest, about Brown and Miss McGawley had been accepted by Catholics; no one controverted or corrected them. Bernard U. Campbell, Charles I. White and Bp. O'Connor repeated them on his authority, and so did Mr. De Courcy. Does that make him responsible alone, and him the author of what Watson wrote?

"The one who corrected Watson and really led to some investigation was Thompson Westcott and you do not mention him at all. It was easy to go to the records that gentleman pointed out, but when De Courcy wrote no local historian, Catholic or Protestant, had done anything to correct Watson.

"You refer to Lambing. When his work was nearly printed Mr. Cannon of the house of Benziger Bros. told me of its plan, and I said that I hoped he was not going to repeat all those statements which had been shown to be incorrect. He wrote to Rev. Mr. Lambing who then went to considerable expense and trouble to get the papers of Mr. Wescott. That he has corrected the old story of Watson is due to my suggestion.

"Now after Westcott printed his correction of Watson, it was easy for Father Jordan, J. Carroll McCaffrey, to say that De Courcy was wrong; but it is dishonest and grossly dishonest to say not a word about Watson, and to ignore Westcott; to make De Courcy responsible for Watson, and to give others the credit due Westcott.

"The date of Westcott's contribution we know; but what investigations Father Jordan made or when, you do not distinctly state, nor do you give the date of Mr. McCaffrey's. If it is made a point that these gentlemen discovered all this before Mr. Westcott, I should like to see distinct and definite proof of it. When he was writing we were in constant correspondence, and I am certain that he will attest that he had no Catholic guide in his researches that exploded Watson's story.

"The book was Mr. De Courcy's and when I added to it a few years ago, I did not rewrite the book or correct everything I knew or felt assured was erroneous. Men like O'Kane Murray had plundered and abused it; I did not purpose to give them new and fresh matter for their nefarious work.

"Where is the distinct proof that Washington and Lafayette never attended a service at St. Joseph's? You say he is merely repeating an error. Where is the proof that it is an error? Copying an error would not make him a romancer, but prove that he was in error.

"Father Jordan is very sweeping in his statement as to De Courcy's dates. They number several hundred. How many has he found erroneous? Are there enough to justify the charge that he is very inaccurate.

"I am very sorry you sent me the slip. It does not impress me favorably.

"Catholic scholars of your city have not so far as I can learn added enough facts as to Catholicity in Philadelphia prior to the Revolution to make a pamphlet of a dozen pages. Yet information must exist if time and pains were taken to unearth them. Miss Elizabeth McGawley's name eluded Mr. Westcott I admit, but she may be no myth. There were priests in Philadelphia before Father Greaton founded the Jesuit mission, but their aliases are unknown to some people.

"I think your antiquarians would do well to bring forward some hitherto unpublished facts, and use some that have been published, instead of assailing the character of Mr. De Courcy.

"Let them bring together as much new matter as he did, and we may pardon them if they occasionally fall into errors."

Griffin took exception also to some of the historical facts the volume gave regarding the early history of the Church in Philadelphia and in reply, Dr. Shea sent to him a page from the *Catholic Herald* for November 10, 1840, containing the report of Dr. Michael O'Connor, then the President of St. Charles Seminary, where all these facts were given. "This was Mr. De Courcy's main authority," Shea wrote, "and to abuse him is to abuse Bishop O'Connor."

The reference to O'Kane Murray in the letter cited above belongs also to the De Courcy-Shea *History*. John O'Kane Murray came with his parents to New York from Ireland as a boy of nine in 1856. After graduating from St. John's College,

Fordham, he studied medicine in the University of the City of New York, and practiced his profession until 1880, when he was stricken with tuberculosis. He then went to Chicago, where he died in 1885. He was a popular contributor to the Catholic periodical press and had already published several volumes in the field of American Catholic history, when the publishing house of the Sadliers suggested that he prepare a *Popular History of the Catholic Church in the United States* (pp. 647), for the approaching Centennial of 1876.

The work lived up to its title in every respect and was uncommonly popular, four editions being issued within six months after its appearance. The *Popular History* suited the year in which it appeared. There is no erudition in the volume, although it abounds in references to sources, some of which are now lost. The appendices and notes in the back are valuable as summaries of all that had been published up to that time on the question of Catholic literature in the United States and on the problem of loss and gain. O'Kane Murray's work showed higher skill in its arrangement than did the Shea translation of De Courcy. Shea could have had no personal share in the composition of a popular book of this nature; in fact in the preface to the first volume of his own *History* (1886), he severely criticises Murray, without, however, mentioning his name, in these terms: "I have given the authorities in my notes, although scholars generally have been compelled to abandon the plan by the dishonesty of those who copy references and pretend to have consulted books and documents they never saw, and frequently could not read." Dr. Shea's works, as is well known, were so systematically pillaged by many authors that for a time he thought seriously of abandoning references altogether.

CHAPTER IV

THE "CRAMOISYS"

(1857-1863)

The discussion aroused by Shea's translation of De Courcy's History has led us a goodly number of years from the last stopping place in our narrative. Dr. Shea had not lost sight of one of his earlier plans in the midst of the work his post with the Dunigans entailed. In 1855 (October 2), he read a paper before the New York Historical Society, entitled *The Life and Character of of Garakonthie, Sachem of Onondaga.* The following year the press of the Society issued his *Narrative of a Captivity among the Mohawk Indians and a Description of New Netherland in 1642-43 by Father Isaac Jogues, S. J., with a Memoir of the holy Missionary* (pp. 69). That same year he published in the Boston *Pilot* an interesting series of papers on *Perils of the Ocean and Wilderness, or Narratives of Shipwrecks and Indian Captivities,* which were gleaned from the annals of the early missionaries and were later published in one volume by Dunigan (1856). This latter volume (pp. 206) was an effort to widen the reading-public of the *Relations* by presenting some of the most graphic accounts of the perils the misssionaries had encountered. A second edition was soon called for, but the book has now become a rarity. Dr. Shea published also this year (1856) a translation of the *Life of the Blessed Virgin Mary, of her Chaste Spouse Saint Joseph, and her holy Parents Saint Joachim and Saint Anne.* The life of the Blessed Virgin was that by Gentilucci; that of St. Joseph was by Father Vallego, a Mexican Jesuit of the seventeenth century, and the lives of Saints Joachim and Anne by Father Binet, S. J.

There are no real dividing lines in the years which followed John Gilmary Shea's retirement from the Society of Jesus in 1852. Year after year he worked away with a thoroughness and a dispatch that was astonishing. "It almost puzzles us," wrote Marc F. Vallette after Shea's death, "to answer the question how did he find time for this voluminous work, spread over so broad a field. Still his historical and archeological studies, though his constant and favorite occupation, in which are his deeper interest was absorbed, did not secure for him a certain and adequate livelihood. Learning is not a financially remunerative calling. A novelist may be paid by the tens of thousands, a historical investigator is frequently glad to find a publisher. The respect paid him may be great, but his income is small."

So it proved with Dr. Shea. He was honored all through the next forty years by every living historian in the United States. Historical Societies also vied to do him honor. While Catholics were slow at first to recognize the splendid apologetical value of Dr. Shea's publications, during the last few years of his life he was placed by his own Church among the illustrious leaders whose names are to be preserved to posterity as among her most brilliant scholars.

In chronicling, however, the works which came from his pen, during these thirty years (1852-1882), unless the reader's attention is drawn to the fact, one important phase of Dr. Shea's life will be missed entirely. In very few of his letters do we find a word of complaint that year in and year out he was forced to labor at things that were trivial and ephemeral compared to the work his genius called him to do. For well-nigh twenty-five years his only steady income came from his salary as editor-in-chief of Frank Leslie's publications, *Popular Monthly, Chimney Corner, Sunday Magazine,* etc. Marc Vallette has written: "For upwards of twenty years a devout, strong, unwavering Catholic published week after week journals chiefly read by Protestants; he never failed in his loyalty to his Faith, he never sacrificed any principles, and yet his Protestant readers found no fault; most of them probably never suspected that they read the matter provided for them by an ex-Jesuit, who to the end of his life remained in spirit a son of Ignatius."

With this part of Dr. Shea's life we have less concern. It enters into the narrative only as a matter of great regret that so brilliant and versatile a scholar did not fall upon better days or at least find in his own Communion leaders far-sighted enough to relieve him of all financial worries. That this was done by some members of the American hierarchy in the closing years of his life only heightens the regret. His *History of the Catholic Church in the United States,* written during the years he received support (1882-1892), is a lasting memorial to what might have been had interest in Catholic historical scholarship been advanced enough all through these years (1852-1882) to have created for him a financial support which would not have embarrassed him and would certainly have honored the leaders of the Church in America.

John Gilmary Shea's historical and literary work during the next quarter of a century (1857-1882) can be regarded from various angles. During these years he belonged by right of his profound scholarship and his numerous publications to that small group of outstanding American historians who were writing between Prescott's death in 1859 and Bancroft's passing in 1891— George Ticknor (1791-1871), Henry C. Lea (1825-1907), John Lothrop Motley (1814-1877), and Francis Parkman (1823-1893). Jared Sparks was the Nestor of American historians in the first part of this middle period, although he published nothing of importance after his *Correspondence of the American Revolution* in 1853. A serious accident in 1851 impaired his right arm and the last years of his life, (he died in 1866) were spent in answering inquiries that came to him from many quarters. Bancroft's *History* continued to appear until 1874; and his *History of the Formation of the Constitution of the United States* was published in 1882. Motley's *History of the United Netherlands* came out between 1860 and 1867, and his *Life and Death of John of Barneveld* in 1874. Parkman's first great work *The Conspiracy of Pontiac* was given to the public in 1851, and the *Pioneers of New France,* in 1865.

After Sparks' death, Parkman was easily the leader in American historical literature. In fact, no American historian has ever equalled Parkman "in sympathy with his subject, in mastery of style, and in fusion of the writer's vigorous character." Bancroft's fitfulness of historical activity became almost a permanency after the publication of the ninth and tenth volumes of his *History* in 1874. Fourteen years separated the eighth and ninth volumes. To this period, however, belongs his great oration on Lincoln (1866). Peter Force passed away in 1868, the great dream of his life, the *American Archives,* unrealized. Edmund Bailey O'Callaghan, with bitterer attacks in the Albany Legislature against his publication of sources than Force experienced in Congress, continued year after year to issue valuable reprints of

archival material until 1871, when circumstances surrounding his work and an accident put an end to his activities.

In point of numbers, Dr. Shea's publications outstrip those of almost all his contemporaries; almost one hundred volumes, some large, others small, besides a long list of historical articles in Catholic and non-Catholic periodicals, coming from his pen during these years under review.

John Gilmary Shea had read and studied for several years the precious collections of original manuscripts which Father Felix Martin, S. J., was assembling in the archives of St. Mary's College, Montreal. He had written on various occasions to Dr. O'Callaghan, when some new and valuable document came into Father Martin' possession and had often expressed his fears that the learned French Jesuit would be too occupied with the administration of the new College to attempt the publication of these sources. After Shea's departure from the Society of Jesus in 1852, Dr. O'Callaghan frequently urged him to make use of his friendship with Father Martin and of his former place in the Society to secure these manuscripts for publication. Shea mentioned the matter several times in his letters to his former superior, but did not find Father Martin enthusiastic over the project of allowing these documents to reach the public through an American. Father Martin, scholar that he was, realized the pleasure an editor would have in bringing them to light. O'Callaghan had experienced so much reluctance in obtaining valuable documents from private archives for his own publications that he continued to advise Shea to use the utmost tact with the Jesuits of Montreal. Frankly, both men felt that the work could best be done, when done by themselves. Up to January, 1855, Shea had not succeeded in persuading Father Martin to loan him a group of the *Relations*. On January 29, 1855, Dr. O'Callaghan writes to his young friend: "I am sorry to learn by yours of the 24th, that you have failed in obtaining the Mss. Worse luck now: better another time. I do not think that he (Martin) suspected you. The truth is, as I foresaw, that they want to print those things yonder (Montreal). You say they'll never do it. *Possible*. But still they look forward to that, and as the good Father has more to expect from Quebec than from New York, 'tis only natural he should await their pleasure . . . . . I do not pretend to be as well able to see through a millstone as you are, but I think you had better lie on your oars. They'll certainly smell a rat, if you continue urging them to comply with your wishes. Besides, *cui bono?* Quebec must pronounce. . . . ."

Meanwhile, quite unexpectedly, the Society of Jesus gave Dr. Shea the required permission to issue a series of reprints of these rare little volumes in their possession. "I congratulate you on your success," wrote Dr. O'Callaghan from Albany, on February 21, 1855, ". . . .hold on to the documents until I go down, which will be in a few days. In proportion to their great value is at the same time their great scarcity. A complete set is not now to be found even in the Royal Library at Paris."

Dr. Shea began the publication of these manuscripts in 1857; and for a period covering thirty years, these little booklets were issued to a chosen number of friends and historical students. One hundred copies only were printed of the two editions which appeared simultaneously, one in octavo and one in duodecimo. The twenty-five volumes published by Shea are now among the *rarissima* of our American libraries.

It was the duty of the Jesuit missionaries in North America to send each year to the superior in Montreal a written account of their labors. As each year reached its close, the Jesuit Superior sent to the Superior in Paris, a redaction of the letters he had received. This summary was called a *Relation,* or narrative of the most important events occurring in the district under his care. From 1632 to 1673, these narratives were carefully edited by the French Superior and were then published from the press of Sebastien Cramoisy. In all, forty volumes were issued and were popular in educated circles. As the years passed, the "Cramoisys" as they were called, became scarcer and scarcer, and, when Dr. O'Callaghan called attention to them in his *Jesuit Relations* (1847), no complete set was known to exist either in Europe or in America. With the assistance of O'Callaghan and Shea, Mr. James Lenox began to collect these rare volumes, and today what is probably the only complete set of "Cramoisys" is in the Lenox Library (Public Library, New York). In 1858, the Canadian government reprinted the "Cramoisys" in three large octavo volumes. This edition is also so scarce that copies are seldom offered for sale.

Dr. Shea's intention was to secure those *Relations,* still in manuscript, which had been prepared for publication after 1672, but which had never seen the light, and to print them as supplementary material to the original set of forty volumes. For that reason, he kept the name and his twenty-five little brochures are known as the *Cramoisy Series.* Both O'Callaghan and Father Martin published similar *Relations;* and with all this material as a basis, Reuben Gold Thwaites published (1896-1901) the travels and explorations of the Jesuit missionaries in New France in the original and in translation under the title *The Jesuit Relations and Allied Documents,* in seventy-three volumes.

Dr. Shea's *Cramoisy Series* is as follows:

1. Gravier (J.), *Relation de la Mission des Illinois* (1693), pp. 65, 1857.
2. Bigot (J.), *Relation de la Mission Abanaquaise* (1864), pp. 61, 1857.
3 Bigot (J.), *Relation de la Mission Abanaquaise* (1865), pp. 21, 1858.
4. Bigot (V.), *Relation de la Mission Abanaquaise* (1701), pp. 34, 1858.
5. Cavalier (R.), *Voyage de M. La Salle* (1865), pp. 54, 1858.
6-7. Chaumonot (J. M.), *Autobiographie,* pp. 108, 1858.
8. Tranchepain (A.), *Voyage des Ursulines à la Nouvelle Orleans,* pp. 62, 1859.
9. *Registres des Baptesmes et Sepultures au Fort Duquesne,* 1753, '54, '55, '56, pp. 51, 1859.
10. *Journal de la Guerre contres les Chicachas, 1739-40,* pp. 92, 1859.
11. Gravier (J.), *Voyage à l'embouchure du Mississippi, 1700,* pp. 68, 1859.
12. Dablon (C.), *Relation de la Nouvelle France, 1673-79,* pp. 290, 1860.
13. Dablon (C), *Relation de la Nouvelle France, 1672-73,* pp. 219, 1861.
14. *Relations diverses sur la bataille du Malenguelé,* pp. 75, 1860.
15. *Relation des Missions du Seminaire de Quebec, 1700,* pp. 66, 1861.
16. Jogues (I.), *Novum Belgium,* pp. 44, 1862.

17. Sagean (M.), *Extrait des Voyages de Matthieu Sagean,* pp. 32, 1863.
18. Milet (P.), *Relation d'une captivité parmi les Onneiouts, 1690-91,* pp. 56, 1864.
19. *Nouvelle France et Nouvelle Angleterre, Negotiations, 1648,* pp. 63, 1866.
20. *Relation des Affaires du Canada en 1696,* pp. 73, 1865.
21. Bigot (J.) *Relation de la Mission Abanaquaise,* 1702, pp. 26, 1865.
22. Gravier (J.), *Lettre sur les Affaires de la Louisiana,* pp. 18, 1865.
23. *Lettre du P. Bigot à Annexy,* pp. 9, 1858.
24. Druilettes (G.), *Epistola ad Joannem Winthrop,* pp. 13, pp. 13, 1864.
25. Gendron, *Quelques Particularitez sur le Pays des Hurons,* pp. 26, 1860.
26. Chauchetière, *La Vie de la B. Catherine Tegahkouita, dictée à present la Sainte Sauvagesse,* Par le Père Claude Chauchetière de la Compagnie de Jesus, pp. 179, 1887.

Shea's *Cramoisy Series* has been unequally estimated by historical scholars. As a pioneer in the field of calling attention to the *Relations* as of prime importance for the student of French colonial America, Dr. Shea has won a unique place in American historiography. The reprinting, however, was not always successful. Victor Paltsits writes anent Dr. Shea's publication of Dablon's *Relation* of 1672-73—"The Shea series is a nebulous output. The volumes were issued without regard to chronological arrangement; not all of them are Jesuit *Relations*—several of the twenty-five which compose the set have no place in a collection of documents relating to the Order; there is seldom any information vouchsafed as to where and when the document was obtained; the editing of the Manuscripts is sometimes most recklessly done, the text being often modernized, and made to suffer from emendations of every character."

Only one who has seen in his correspondence the long train of petty annoyances which disturbed Dr. Shea's peace during the years of the *Cramoisy Series* (1857-1887) can give the proper answer to Dr. Paltsits' criticism. The *Cramoisy Series* was a private publication of a scholar who knew better than any histor-

ian of his time, not even with the exception of Parkman, the missionary history of the priests of New France. He took every
care to reproduce the *Relations* exactly as he found them. But
it was only by a kind of running warfare between himself and
Munsell, the printer, that the little works appeared even as well
done as they were. One *Relation,* in fact, was so badly repro-
duced by Munsell, that it had to be destroyed and a new edition
printed. Dr. O'Callaghan repeatedly urged Shea to give up Munsell, but it was a question of economy for a scholar who had no
financial help whatever for this ideal design. American Catholics
were sublimely indifferent to the question of preserving these old
records from destruction; and, if the truth can be told, Shea
himself during these years was a pawn in the hands of unscrup-
ulous Catholic publishers of New York, who looked upon him
merely as a brilliant and swift composer or compiler of popular
books for the trade.

Poverty sat behind Shea's shoulder all through these middle
years, and there are pages in his business relations with certain
Catholic publishers which had best be allowed to pass into oblivion. "I do not pity you, working night and day," O'Callaghan
wrote on July 9, 1855, "don't you know that if you will let them,
these Devilish Booksellers will flay you in order to make a drum
afterwards of your skin to rattle your praise on with your shin
bones for drumsticks! What nice music that will be for the
Widow Shea! Have sense, child, don't be in a hurry to coin your
heartstrings into gold. Take some recreation, but don't take it
until next month, when, perhaps Providence in its wise dispensa-
tions, may bring us once more together."

Three other volumes belong to the year 1857. The first of these
is the translation of Tachet de Barneval's *Histoire Légendaire de
l'Irlande,* which had been published in Paris, in 1856. The story
of Irish history was attracting scholarly attention about this time
in the United States. The treasures locked up in manuscripts
were then beginning to be presented to the reading public, and
there was a renaissance of interest in Ireland's past. Prejudices,
however, were still in evidence in the field of Irish hagiography,
and Dr. Shea believed that Tachet de Barneval had written an
account of the saints of Erin which would appeal to English
readers. The translation has kept the rich, exuberant style of

the original, and is as graceful a narrative as ever came from Shea's pen. He was at the time, as he says in the preface, "rashly perhaps, engaged on a Life of St. Patrick, which he hopes soon to complete in spite of the difficulty of obtaining here works on the early Church history of Ireland." Dr. Shea's *Life of St. Patrick* was never published, but is among his papers in manuscript. Another unfinished manuscript is his *History of the Society of Jesus*. The *Legendary History of Ireland* (pp. 308) was followed by a translation of Canon Parenty's *Life of Saint Angela Merici of Brescia, foundress of the Order of Saint Ursula* (pp. 251). To this translation Dr. Shea appended the first history of the Ursulines in Ireland, Canada, and the United States. A little publication in eighteen pages appeared also in 1857, Father Gabriel Druillettes' *Journal of An Embassy from Canada to the United Colonies of New England in 1610*, which Shea translated from the original manuscript and published in the *Collections* of the New York Historical Society.

The following year (1858) Shea published a *Seraphic Manual* and a translation of Father Johann Roothann's *Method of Meditation*. This same year he began his long editorship (1858-1890) of the *General Catholic Directory, Almanac and Ordo*. Dunigan was its publisher from 1858 to 1862. The annual volumes from 1864 to 1896 came from the house of Sadlier.

The *Catholic Directory* has broken more than one editor's spirit in the long years of its existence. Issued first in 1817 by Matthew Field, in New York, the *Catholic Laity's Directory to the Church Service* was a failure and was not continued, although it had been announced as an annual publication. The failure was not due to the lack of financial support, but to the lack of interest taken by the clergy who neglected to send information concerning their labors. Five years later (1822), another attempt was made, the *Laity's Directory to the Church Service*, published by William H. Creagh. This failed for the same reason. A third venture was the *United States Catholic Almanac or Laity's Directory*, begun in 1832 by James Myers, of Baltimore. From 1833 to 1837, annual *Directories* were issued by Myers, and from 1838 to 1854 by Fielding Lucas, Jr., of the same city. The 1858 edition was published by Dunigan & Kirker, with Dr. Shea as general editor. In 1859, Murphy, the publisher of Baltimore, published

a rival volume, *The Metropolitan Catholic Allmanac,* begun, as
is stated in the preface, at the request of the Archbishop of Baltimore.   In 1860, the two rival publications were issued, Dunigan's in New York, Murphy's in Baltimore.   In 1861, only Murphy's *Almanac* made its appearance.   No general *Directory* was
issued for 1862 or 1863, owing to the Civil War.   In 1864, again
under Dr. Shea's editorship, the *Directory* appeared from the
press of the Sadliers.   From 1864 to 1885, the Sadliers had the
field to themselves.   In 1886 the Hoffmans of Milwaukee began
a rival publication, on account of the dissatisfaction caused by
"the inaccuracy, incompleteness and exhorbitant price" of the
Sadlier *Directory.*   The two *Directories* came out annually until
1896, when the Sadliers ceased publishing their volume.   Hoff-
mann continued alone in the field until 1897, when the *Directory*
plant was purchased by the Wiltzius firm.   From 1897 to 1911
the house of Wiltzius issued the *Directory* and it was then sold
to Messrs. P. J. Kenedy & Sons of New York, who have published it since 1912.

The preface of all these volumes repeats the same tale: reports
and statistics were difficult to obtain from bishops and chancel-
lors; so much so that it can hardly be said that any one annual
volume presents an absolutely accurate statement of the Catholic
Church in the United States.

Dr. Shea's correspondence during these forty-two years of
editorship of the *Directory* has its share of letters complaining
about the statistics given for some of the dioceses.   In spite of
all his efforts, his appeals in many dioceses, including that of
New York, were often overlooked and the old statistics had to
stand.   The work was tedious and not very remunerative.   He
was encouraged often by quaint letters from Dr. O'Callaghan,
who admitted in one of his missives: "When I get home in the
evening, I am as stupid as an owl (owls *are* stupid, you know,
for those of them I ever saw wore glasses) and have scarcely
brains enough to bless myself, which I should hardly be able to
do, were it not that I was taught long ago, and the mechanism
remains."   On another occasion to stir Shea up he said, "Eleazar
Williams, the lost prince, wants to know: Who is this Shea?"
Dr. Shea had dealt rather summarily with the "Lost Dauphin" in
his translation of De Courcy.   On another occasion, when Dr.

Shea was rather depressed over the *Directory,* O'Callaghan advised him to get out more into the open and to learn how to play. "Do you remember," he writes, "the holidays when a schoolboy? I do not believe you do. When I first knew you, you were as big as you are now, so I believe you never were a boy, but like Jonah's gourd, were as big when you were born as you have ever been since. But if ever you were a boy and had holidays, you can foreshadow my week, at Mrs. O'C's expense!"

Dr. Shea was pleasantly surprised about this time with two letters, one in Latin, the other in French, from Cardinal Bedini, thanking him for the splendid volume De Courcy and himself had written, and in which, as we have seen, there is a rather extended dedication to the celebrated nuncio. "Que de peines," Bedini writes, "que vous vous êtes données pour l'autre livre de M. Courcy dans lequel on parle si bien de ma Mission aux Etats-Unis!"

It was about this time, also, that Shea was contemplating the publication of a series of grammars and dictionaries in the North American Indian languages. While on the trail of one of these manuscripts, O'Callaghan blandly informed him: "Mr. O'Loughlin thinks a Priest has borrowed it. If so, then I despair of seeing it again, my experience of these Gents is that they do not subscribe to the doctrine of Restitution of Books. Possibly, they are more particular about Umbrellas." It was by some of the Catholic priests of the country that Dr. Shea was being attacked for statements which appeared in his De Courcy translation and also for the absence of certain traditional "facts" which Shea disregarded as unhistorical. Dr. O'Callaghan was able to dispel his sense of injury with clippings from the Albany *Statesman,* where his own great work for the history of New York State was being bitterly attacked by the Know-Nothings—"Frères Ignorantins"—on account of the many Catholic documents which were appearing in his volume.

In a letter, dated Albany March 7, 1857, O'Callaghan gives a curious side-light on the intolerance that had crept into New York political life: "The foundation of all is those Notes to vol. IX. and ascribing the Honor of discovering the Salt Springs to the Jesuits. And now to show how these things are brought to bear. I have only to mention what has recently been told me by a Gentleman (an American) of the highest respectability here. When Dr. Beck's approaching death rendered it necessary to look out for a Successor, my informant was consulted, and, as he says, at once mentioned by name, on grounds unnecessary to mention here, but such as may naturally be entertained. He was met at once by an awful shake of the head, an explanation of which was demanded. 'Oh! he'll never do. He's a Jesuit!' The gentleman who was making this communication to me then gravely asked me if I were indeed of that Order?" The clipping enclosed by Dr. O'Callaghan from the *Statesman* accuses the *Documentary History* as being "characterized in many portions by a bitterness of feeling towards all Protestant sects."

On January 5, 1858, Dr. O'Callaghan wrote to Shea recommending that, instead of a supplement on a topic which Shea intended to treat in a forthcoming edition of De Courcy, a separate volume be written entitled *The Catholic Writers of America.* "Be careful," he says, "how you mention it to anyone, for ten to one but some fellow will execute it before you." There is nothing in Shea's papers to suggest that he ever began this work, though it may have been the incentive to another, the outlines of which he left incomplete, *The Glories of the Catholic Church,* the subtitle being, "her great saints, popes, bishops, missionaries, churches, abbeys, statesmen, warriors, scholars, poets, artists, men of science, architects, explorers, inventors, religious orders, musicians, educators, and doers of works of mercy." He did however edit a volume with this title, which was published by Thomas Kelly in 1877. The subjects treated were taken from Shea's list. Shea was trying at the time to have Cardinal Manning write the first chapter on the great popes and their influence, and to secure Dr. Newman for the chapter on the great bishops.

It is not certain what it was in Dr. Shea's plans at this time which secured for him the following recommendation from Archbishop Hughes:

"New York, Feby. 13, 1858.

"The undersigned hereby certifies, that John Gilmary Shea, is a Catholic gentleman of exemplary life, and extensive, as well as varied erudition. He has already rendered great service to the Catholic religion in the country, by his research and publications in reference to the early missions and missionarys of this country. I know of no other writer, to whom copies of historical documents, whether, in the Archives of Rouen, or elsewhere, could be intrusted with so much prospect of their being used for the best purposes of religion.

✠*John, Abp. of New York"*

A curious incident happened this same year which emphasizes the similarity of tastes of the two men, who had mutually encouraged and inspired each other for about a decade of years. In March, 1858, Dr. O'Callaghan wrote to Shea, asking him for information regarding the earliest Catholic Bibles printed in this country, for a brochure he was then preparing, and which eventually he published in 1861 with the title, *List of Editions of the Holy Scriptures and Parts Thereof, Printed in America Previous to 1860.* This was suggested by James Lenox, to whom the *List* is inscribed. O'Callaghan's volume contains "a magnificent introduction, which shows what an amount of information with regard to colonial conditions of all kinds O'Callaghan had collected and digested. Besides being a veritable mine of exact information, however, this introduction is very interesting reading, because it gives some idea of the difficulties under which the early printers and publishers labored."

Dr. Shea was amazed at the request of March 26, and replied at once that he had been quietly working for several years on a *Bibliographical Account of Catholic Bibles, Testaments, and other portions of Scripture, translated from the Latin Vulgate and printed in the United States,* and that it was almost ready for the printer. On March 31, Dr. O'Callaghan replied: "I am sorry that my request for those Bibles shocked you. You sent me a list once, but I passed it to Mr. Lenox. Now, at the request of that gentleman, I have prepared a Paper on the early editions of the Bible in this country, but I have confined myself to *first* editions. This paper is complete as far as I shall go, with the exception of the Catholic Bible. Therefore please send me your copy of Carey Stewart & Co. 1790 ed., which I shall return after a few days. I would not like my Paper to go, without adding the Catholic Bible. I should like to say, also, when the first Catholic Bible was printed in Baltimore and New York, if you could give me date & printer's name. But I do not wish to interfere with your purpose of getting up a bibliographical account, as you can do more in judgment on others. Let me hear your opinion on this plan & view of the case."

All through the year 1858, both Dr. Shea and his wife were ill, and there are among his letters many consoling messages from Albany from Dr. O'Callaghan and Mrs. O'Callaghan encouraging them both in their predicament. Once O'Collaghan wrote:

"Les Geux
Sont des gens heureux—
Compared with us quill-drivers!"

Financially New York was not proving all that Dr. Shea expected. He was not able to support his little family in comfort, nor could he give Mrs. Shea the care and medical attention she needed, because of this constant lack of money. He began correspondence with a Philadelphia firm, hoping to secure a more lucrative position, and announced what he thought to be his approaching departure to Dr. O'Callaghan. On April 20, 1858, O'Callaghan wrote: "Mrs. O'C. says, you might as well be in St. Petersburg or the Moon for any chance I stand of ever again meeting you." If only Shea had gone to Paris, O'Callaghan said he would not be troubled, "but Philadelphia? Well, Good-bye!" A week later, at Mrs. O'Callaghan's suggestion, he wrote again: "You're overworked, good friend, and need relaxation. Besides Mrs. Shea wants the house cleaned and you're in the way; so come to Albany for a visit." The invitation was not heeded, and on May 9, in a letter to Dr. Shea, he writes: "Dear Mrs. Shea, where's John's carpet bag Please put a couple of shirts in it and turn him out of doors!"

The summer brought a slight change in Dr. Shea's fortunes. He succeeded in extricating himself from a fatiguing and unsatisfactory position with the Dunigans and in forming a better business connection which was more to his liking and which promised to be eventually a source of profit to himself. Towards the end of the year, Archbishop Hughes appointed him a member of an Historical Commission for the Archdiocese of New York:

New York, Dec. 30, 1858.
"Dear Sir:

"I have taken the liberty of appointing you as one of three members, who are to constitute what I call the Bureau of Records,

JOHN GILMARY SHEA AT THE AGE OF FORTY MRS. JOHN GILMARY SHEA (1863)

in connection with the building of the New Cathedral. The object will be, to preserve from the beginning such memoirs in connection with our great work as you yourself have desired in your searches for early historical information connected with the origin, either of missions or of churches in this great and growing country of ours. Some unborn historian of the Catholic Church in the United States will pray for the prolongation of your life or the repose of your soul, for having contributed to leave behind data, from which he may complete his Ecclesiastical history of the U. S. with less toil and more satisfaction than you have experienced in your attempts hitherto. And in view of such circumstances, you can say our *hand ignavus mali miseris succurere disco.*

> *"Yours Very Faithfully in Christ,*
> ✠JOHN, *Abp. of New York.*

Dr. Shea was proud of this signal honor and ever afterwards looked upon his post as that of diocesan historiographer. In fact he so refers to himself in the preface to a large volume he published on *The Catholic Churches of New York City, with Sketches of their History and Lives of the present Pastors,* which appeared in 1879.

In 1860, Shea began the publication of a series of valuable reprints to which he gave the title: *Library of American Linguistics.* These volumes were similar in design with the *Cramoisy Series.* The *Linguistics* were to contain grammars, dictionaries, and vocabularies of the Indian tribes of North America, and the sources were to be unpublished manuscripts in French, German, Spanish, and Latin, of the early missionaries and others. His purpose was to preserve these languages in as pure a form as possible before they were lost. The study of American ethnology had been fettered by the want of anything like reliable grammars and dictionaries, and so long as students were obliged to rely on scanty or erroneous vocabularies, the science remained in its infancy. The *Library* was recognized at the time as a signal service to American ethnologists. Dr. Shea published fifteen of these volumes, some small, others large, in editions of one hundred copies and presented them to friends and scholars. Thirteen of them were printed between 1861 and 1864; the other two appeared in 1873-1874.

The volumes published were:

1. Shea, J. G. *A French-Onondaga Dictionary, from a manuscript of the seventeenth century,* pp. 103, New York, 1860. MS. in Georgetown College Library.
2. Mengarini, Gregory. *A Selfish or Flathead Grammar,* pp. viii-122. New York, 1861.
3. Smith, Buckingham. *A Grammatical Sketch of the Heve Language,* translated from an unpublished Spanish manuscript, pp. 26. New York, 1861.
4. Arroyo De La Cuesta, Felipe. *Grammar of the Mutsun Language, spoken at the mission of San Juan Bautista, Alta California,* pp. viii-48. New York, 1861.
5. Smith, Buckingham. *Grammar of the Pima or Vevome, a language of Sonora, from a manuscript of the eighteenth century.* Pp. viii-97. *Doctrina Christiana y Confesionario en Lengua Nevome, Sea La Pima, propria de Sonora.* Pp. 32. New York, 1862.
6. Pandosy. *Grammar and Dictionary of the Yakama Language.* Pp. viii-97. New York 1862.
7. Sitjar, Bonaveuture. *Vocabulary of the Language of San Antonio* Mission, California. Pp. xix-53. New York, 1861.
8. Arroyo De La Cuesta. *A Vocabulary or Phrase Book of Mutsun Language of Alta California.* Pp. viii-96. New York, 1862.
9. Bruyas, James. *Radical Words of the Mohawk Language, with their derivatives.* Pp. 123, New York, 1862.
10. Gibbs, George. *Alphabetical Vocabularies of the Clallam and Lummi.* Pp. viii-40. New York, 1863.
11. Gibbs, George. *A Dictionary of the Chinook Jargon, or, Trade Language of Oregon.* Pp. xiv-43. New York, 1863.
13. Maillard, Abbé. *Grammar of the Mikmaque Language of Nova Scotia, edited from manuscripts by Rev. Joseph M. Bellinger.* Pp. 101. New York, 1864.
14. Matthews, Washington. *Grammar and Dictionary of the Language of the Hidatsi (Minnestarees, Grosventres of the Missouri),* with an introductory sketch of the tribe. Pp. xxv-148. New York, 1873.

CHAPTER V

THE MIDDLE YEARS

(1863-1882)

After the outbreak of the Civil War, Dr. Shea projected a series of volumes, which he entitled *Fallen Brave: a biographical Memorial of the American Officers who have given their lives for the preservation of the Union.* Only one volume was published (1861), containing twenty-four biographies. The majority of these he wrote and the others he edited. Among the lives is that of Colonel Lowe, of Batavia, Ohio, who won an uneviable reputation after the Mexican War as the American officer who brought what was believed to be a consecrated Host from the battlefield and kept it in a Church of England prayer book where in January, 1849, it was found by Archbishop Purcell, who consumed It.

During the war, Dr. Shea published: the *Micmac Recollect Hieroglyphics* in the *Historical Magazine* (Vol. V, pp. 289-292); *Chicago from 1673 to 1725, or what is known of the first half-Century of its History,* a communication to the Chicago Historical Society; *Christopher Columbus and Beatrice Enriques,* in the *Historical Magazine* (Vol. V, pp. 225-226); Dablon's *Relation of the Discovery of the South Sea by the Rivers of New France (ibid.,* pp. 237-239); an *Historical Sketch of the Tionontates (ibid.,* pp. 262-269); *Early Voyages Up and Down the Mississippi by Cavalier Le Suer, Gravier, and Guignas, with an Introduction and Notes* (Pp. 191, Albany, 1891)—the edition being limited to one hundred copies; a *Description of the Province and City of New York in 1695* (pp. 127, New York, 1882); *Operations of the French Fleet under Count DeGrasse* (1781-82), pp. 216, New York, 1864; *Affairs at port Chartres* (1768-81). Pp. 12, 1864; *The Lincoln Memorial* (pp. 268), a record of the life, assassination, and obsequies of the martyred President, which he edited and published in 1865; the *Capuchin Missions in Maine,* in the *Historical Magazine* (Vol. VIII, pp. 177, 301), giving an account of the copper plate found at Castine in 1864; and *Early Southern Tracts: A Relation of the successful beginnings of the Lord Baltimore's plantation in Maryland, and Sot-Weed Factor, or a Voyage to Maryland,* both published in 1865.

In addition to all these works, Dr. Shea assisted in editing (1855-1867) the *Historical Magazine.*

In 1865, Shea was at work on a translation of Charlevoix' *History and General Description of New France,* which he published in six volumes from 1866 to 1872.

In 1866, Dr. Shea moved with his family to Elizabeth, N. J., where he found quiet for the difficult and tedious work of this translation. It was for this scholarly work that Dr. Shea received the highest praise bestowed on any of his books. One review deserves to be cited here:

"The spirit and the manner in which Mr. Shea has entered upon his task are above all praise. It is with him a 'labor of love.' In these days of literary 'jobs,' when bad translating and careless editing are palmed off on the amateurs of choice books in all the finery of broad margins and faultless typography, it is refreshing to meet with a book of which the mechanical excellence is fully equaled by the substantial value of its contents, and by the thorough, conscientious and scholarlike character of the literary execution. The labor and the knowledge bestowed on this translation would have sufficed to produce an original history of high merit. Charlevoix rarely gives his authorities. Mr. Shea has more than supplied this deficiency. Not only has he traced out the sources of his author's statements and exhibited them in notes, but he has had recourse to sources of which Charlevoix knew nothing. He is thus enabled to substantiate, correct or amplify the original narrative. He translates it, indeed, with literal precision, but in his copious notes he sheds such a flood of new light upon it that this translation is of far more value to the student than the original work. Since Charlevoix's time, many documents unknown to him, though bearing on his subject, have been discovered, and Mr. Shea has diligently availed himself of them. The tastes and studies of many years have made him familiar with this field of research, and prepared him to accomplish an undertaking which would otherwise have been impracticable."

were italicized: in the New, quotations from the Old Testament also. I have made only the supplied words italic, and used all care to denote all such words."

Then follows a long list of the *errata* in Challoner's Bible, from Genesis to the acts. It is an amazing specimen of philological lore. Only one who possessed a unique grasp of the Latin Vulgate could have detected all the words and phrases which were not English equivalents to St. Jerome's translation. "In concluding this statement of what I consider the most important work of my life," Shea says, "I feel confident that as now submitted to your Grace, this edition of Challoner's Bible is the only one preserving his text, adhering to the Vulgate in all cases, heretofore disfigured by omissions and misprints, and adhering to it in the division of versions, punctuation and orthography, and noting exactly words introduced to complete the sense."

Dr. Shea met with one of the saddest disappointments in his life, when the house of Sadlier issued the Pocket Bible, bearing the Archbishop's *imprimatur,* but without Shea's name on the title page or in the foreword. Dr. Shea honestly wanted the public credit he knew his labors deserved; and he confesses to the Archbishop in a letter dated February 4, 1871, that "the credit and responsibility was the chief inducement for my undertaking the task, not the pittance Mr. Sadlier offered, and finally in his usually unjust and oppressive way, refused to pay me. I do not wish to obtrude on Your Grace my troubles and difficulties, or Lazarus-like, show myself at the rich man's door begging not for alms but for the promised remuneration for my labor; but you can form litle idea of the agony I suffered last year with a dying relative to support and minister to and my own family needs besides and unable to obtain from Mr. Sadlier a single dollar, although he had promised to give me some if I required it; and then when the work was complete he told me that he would not pay part of my claim unless a court of law compelled him and thus avoided paying me a single dollar. He has now an approbation page printed in which being without the preliminary approbation originally given, I am ignored and a notice of copyright in his own name inserted so as to prevent, if possible, my doing for any other any part of my work again, the fruit of years of study and comparison. As it stands I feel that it is unjust to me. I certainly am not one who has sought to thrust myself forward into public notice but in this case feeling that in what I have done to reform the careless Bible printing so long in vogue and especially in this case, I have done perhaps the only service to the Church which is of any real merit, the blow is hard to bear. Do I ask too much of your Grace when I respectfully solicit that you will adapt the present Approbation as to give me credit for my labor or request. Mr. Sadlier to print the other approbation also and at the same time to desist from assuming to copyright my literary labor"?

Dr. Shea broke off all business relations with the Sadliers when this injustice was not immediately removed. Later, credit was given to him for his revision of Challoner, and in a second edition of the Pocket Bible (1876) he added a translation from Allioli's Commentary.

Between 1869 and the appearance of his next important translation, Le Clercq's *First Establishment of the Faith in New France,* which he published in two volumes in 1881, Dr. Shea issued the following works: a new edition of George Alsop's *Character of the Province of Maryland* (No. 5 of Gowans' *Bibliotheca Americana*), which was published in an edition of two hundred copies octavo and sixty-four copies quarto, in 1869; a third edition of his *General History of Modern Europe,* in 1870; a popular work in three large volumes entitled *A Child's History of the United States;* filled with attractive illustrations, which appeared in 1872; the *Life of Pius IX and the Great Events in the History of the Church during his Pontificate* (pp. 440), New York, 1877; his *Catholic Chronicles of New York City (1878),* which has been mentioned above; a revised and augmented edition of the De Courcy-Shea *History of the Catholic Church in the United States,* in 1879, in which are omitted the dedication to Bedini and all the documents relating to the nuncio; and finally what many scholars consider one of the most important volumes in the wide range of his historical activities, Hennepin's *Description of Louisiana,* with a *Bibliography of Hennepin's Works,* which was published towards the end of the year 1880, the bi-centennial of Father Hennepin's exploration of the upper Mississippi and discovery of the Falls of Anthony.

Jacobus Roosevelt Bayley Dei et Apostolicae Sedis gratia, Archiepiscopus Baltimorensis Omnibus has visuris Salutem in D°. Praesentium tenore testamur Latori harum, Domino Joanni Gilmary Shea a plurimis annis nobis notissimo, Catholicae Religionis cultori eximio, litterarum multum perito, ita integro ut fides ei tuto habeatur, et jam nunc de parante ad conscribendam Ecclesiae Americanae historiam, sine periculo aliquo committi posse quaecumque manuscripta, Epistolas, effigies utpote caute ab eo custodienda, ac remittenda, omnes quos aditurus est, precamur ut benigne eum suscipere, eique pro viribus auxilio esse velint. — Datum ex aedibus Episcopalibus Baltimorae VIII Idus Septembris anno Domini 1876.

Jacobus Roosevelt Bayley
Archiep. Baltimorens.

ARCHBISHOP BAYLEY'S LETTER TO SHEA (1876)

During this decade (1869-1880) Dr. Shea was active in other directions. On May 31, 1878, he was invited by the Missouri Historical Society to come to St. Louis for the 205th anniversary of the exploration of the Mississippi River, which was held on July 17 of that year. The invitation is signed by Albert Todd, P. L. Foy, James O. Broadhead, Rt. Rev. Bishop Ryan (later Archbishop of Philadelphia), Mayor Overstolz, and Alexander J. P. Garesché. The resolution passed by the executive council of the Society (June 10, 1878), which accompanied the invitation reads as follows: "Whereas John Gilmary Shea of New York, a corresponding member of this Society, has devoted a life-time to the study of the early history of the United States and especially of Canada and the Valley of the Mississippi, and earned an honorable fame by the books he has written, published, or edited, relating thereto, it is furthermore directed that he be invited to honor our jubilee meeting with his presence and favor the Society with a discourse on the occasion."

This was Dr. Shea's first journey to the west. The address he delivered on the occasion was later published in pamphlet form (pp. 20), in New York.

As we shall see, Dr. Shea was not to wait for the invitation of the prelates of the Third Plenary Council (1884) to begin the greatest work of his life, his *History of the Catholic Church in the United States.* Already in 1878, the plan of the work was taking shape in his mind, and there are letters in his correspondence showing that he was then completing his source-collection for the project. On September 15, 1887, he wrote to R. R. Elliott, of Detroit: "I am one of the few Old Mortalities among our Catholic folk and like to see mementoes of our predecessors in the Faith preserved. But to my regret, I find very, very little preserved as I should wish. Detroit has had a chapel and church since 1701. Is there any old chalice, ciborium, monstrance, or vestment of the French era still kept, or have all disappeared? Are there even tombstones of any of the earlier priests? In Maryland, where Catholicity has existed since 1634, you can scarcely find a trace to show that it was there even in the eighteenth century, and nothing of the seventeenth."

He began also at this time to collect diocesan statutes and syondal *acta et decreta,* and it is significant that at that date, some of the bishops of important Sees were obliged to confess that not a single copy of these valuable sources could be found.

In preparation for the *History,* his correspondence became very large, including the foremost historical scholars here and abroad. There is a pathetic reply from Brother Henry Foley, dated London, November 18, 1880, in which that indefatigable compiler writes: "I am struggling with blindness, from cataract, and am now awaiting an operation." William J. Onahan of Chicago, who possessed all of Shea's great love of the American Church, wrote on December 3, 1880: "I wish your work and works met a wider appreciation and a more prompt recognition in money value. But your labors though warmly appreciated by the studious few will come into greater and wider fame in the hereafter time. Catholics especially owe you a debt of gratitude (of which few of them now seem to comprehend the magnitude) in that you are constantly bringing together the Catholic sources of American history and vindicating their faith before the world."

The publication of Le Clercq (1881) in the same handsome binding and type as his Hennepin's *Description of Louisiana* brought delight to all book-lovers. Father Christian Le Clercq's *First Establishment of the Faith in New France,* published in Paris in 1691, was one of the very rarest Americana. It had never been reprinted in French nor had it been translated in any other language up to Shea's time. Only a few copies of the original were known to bibliophiles, and Shea decided to translate it in a limited edition of two hundred and fifty copies. A sketch of Father Le Clercq's life and labors prefaces the two volumes, and wherever the text needs it, notes and references to the author's statements are given with Shea's accustomed accuracy and fulness. Few of Dr. Shea's works were so eagerly sought for as this.

In 1881, Dr. Shea prepared a *History of the Church in America* (pp. 313-426) as a supplement to Dr. Brennan's translation of Businger's *Christ in His Church: a Catholic Church History* (pp. 426), which Benziger published that year. The following year appeared Dr. Shea's translation of *The Expedition of Don Diego Dionisio De Peñalosa,* which was to win for him a rare honor, that of being the first American to be elected to the Real Academia de Historia of Madrid.

Other bibliographical data may be added to the account already given for these middle years of Dr. Shea's life. Among these are: the *Early History of the Catholic Church in New England,* which appeared in the Boston *Pilot* in 1856, and which he rewrote and augmented for the *Historical Magazine* (Vol. 5, pp. 313, 391); *Early Missions in Acadia,* which was published in the *Catholic World* for February and March, 1871; the *Early Life of Father Chaumonot,* in the same periodical for August 1872; the *First Attempt to Settle Virginia,* read before the New York Historical Society, October 1, 1872; the *Memoir of Buckingham Smith,* in the appendix to Smith's *Narrative of Alva Nuñez Cabeza de Vaca,* New York, 1873; a long series of articles on the Indian Tribes and discoveries of North America, contributed to Appleton's *American Cyclopedia,* between 1874 and 1882; *The Log Chapel on the Rappahannock; the first Christian Shrine in the Old Dominion,* in the *Catholic World* for March, 1875; *The Catholic Church in American History,* a Centennial article in the *American Catholic Quarterly Review,* for the first number, January, 1876; *The Inquisition (ibid.,* April, 1876); *What the Church and the Popes have done for the Science of Geography (ibid.,* October, 1876); *Discovery of the Mississippi River,* in the Wisconsin Historical Society *Collections* (Vol. 7, p. 111); *Romance and Reality of the Death of Father James Marquette, and the Recent Discovery of His Remains,* in the *Catholic World,* for November, 1877; *What the United States Owes to James II,* in the *American Catholic Quarterly Review,* for April, 1877; *The Blue Laws of Connecticut (ibid.,* July, 1877); *The Jewish Element in the Church—a Proof of its Apostolic Origin (ibid.,* October, 1878); *The Catholic Church in the United States in the Recent Translation of Alzog (ibid.,* January, 1789); *The Rapid Increase of the Dangerous Classes in the United States (ibid.,* April, 1879); *The Canadian Element in the United States (ibid.,* October, 1879); *A Pioneer of the West: Rev. Charles Nerinckx (ibid.,* July, 1880); *The Earliest Discussion of the Catholic Question in New England (ibid.,* April, 1881); and *The Early Franciscan Missions in this Country (ibid.,* January, 1882).

On June 25, 1879, St. John's College, Fordham, conferred on John Gilmary Shea the honorary degree of Doctor of Laws. He had long been known, however, as Doctor Shea, due to the honor-

ary degree of J. U. D., conferred upon him by St. Francis Xavier
College, New York City, on July 7, 1862. Honors, as the historical worker counts them, came frequently from 1860 to 1882
in the shape of election to over twenty-five historical, literary and
scientific Societies throughout the country. In many cases, his
was the only Catholic name in the register of these Societies.

These middle years of his life were the maturing period of his
genius. In 1882, he had reached his fifty-eighth birthday. His
health was no better and no worse than it had ever been, and the
strange fact in his life, as much a surprise to himself as to his
friends, was how he was able, in the midst of so many literary
occupations upon which his sustenance and that of his family
depended, to accomplish so much of permanent historical value.
He had worked in the field of American Catholic history as no
American before his time. No fact in the long stretch of years
back to the days when Greenland boasted its line of medieval
bishops, and even beyond that epoch to the misty legends surrounding St. Brendan and his companions, was unknown to this
indefatigable delver into our Catholic past.

Looking backward over these thirty years (1852-1882), much
that Dr. Shea wrote seems disparate in nature and uneven in
value; but he was providentially guided, for when the day came
to go out into the field he had ploughed and planted, there was a
harvest awaiting him which no one but himself was able to reap.

CHAPTER VI

THE HARVEST

(1882-1886)

For six years (1876-1882) Dr. Shea had been working away quietly among his papers and documents, putting all his sources in order and planning his *History of the Catholic Church in the United States*. As early as September 1876, he had asked Archbishop Bayley, of Baltimore, for a letter of recommendation to all who possessed archival material for his purpose. The Archbishop's letter was a source of much encouragement to Dr. Shea, and it opened many archives to him here and abroad. Two years later (April 26, 1878), he wrote to Cardinal Gibbons who had succeeded Dr. Bayley as Archbishop of Baltimore, and it is evident from his letter that he was far advanced in the composition of his first volume:

"Your Grace:-

"I ascertain that the materials collected during a lifetime of research by the late Rev. Charles I. White, D. D., who honored me with a friendly correspondence maintained for years, are by his will to be deposited, as they should be in all propriety, in the Archives of the Cathedral of Baltimore.

"Laboring myself for years in the same field as that learned priest, I hoped to see his work appear, but years went by, and I at last felt that age would prevent his putting the finishing touches.

"My own studies and collections, interrupted and broken up for some years have been resumed, and I have gone over the English, French and Spanish Colonial period more thoroughly than any one before me, always excepting Dr. White's Maryland collection, which I could not pretend to approach in my researches.

"This will now be under Your Grace's control, and I most respectfully solicit permission to examine it for my *History of the Catholic Church in the United States*.

"Unfortunately I have not enjoyed the advantage of personal acquaintance or correspondence with Your Grace as I have with your three immediate predecessors, and I apply to Your Grace as comparatively a stranger, almost tempted to enclose a facsimile of a letter of Archbishop Bayley's, which I have used to intro-duce me to many Archbishops and Bishops in French and Spanish parts. Dr. White's papers are not yet, I presume, in Your Grace's hands, but my request will not, I hope, be deemed premature.

"Your Grace's most ob'd't Servant in Xt

"JOHN GILMARY SHEA."

"Most Rev. James Gibbons, D.D."

Bishop Gilmour of Cleveland was apparently the first of our hierarchy to suggest that Dr. Shea give up all other tasks and be selected by the bishops as official historiographer of the Church in the United States. Dr. Shea was too diffident, however, about his ability to satisfy the bishops in so important a work and preferred as he said to carry it through in a private capacity. "You must not make me *aubulare in magnis aut in mirabilibus supra me,*" he wrote to Bishop Gilmour, on April 20, 1882, "for if God wishes me to do the work, I shall accomplish it; but if I am like the Jewish soldiers who went out unbidden, I shall only prove that I was not selected for the work."

A remarkable tribute was paid Dr. Shea at the eighth annual Convention of the Catholic Young Men's National Union, held at Boston, on May 11, 1882. A set of engrossed resolutions, signed by the President of the Union, Bishop John J. Keane, of Richmond, later first Rector of the Catholic University of Amer-ica, reads as follows:

"Whereas the formation of a sound Catholic literature, es-pecially in the field of history, for the refutation of current errors and the dissemination of right knowledge, is one of the most efficient means of doing honor to the Church of God; and,

"Whereas John Gilmary Shea, LL.D., by his long continued, conscientious, and distinguished labors in this great work, has conferred incalculable benefit on the cause of Catholic truth, and shown himself a model worthy of the imitation of all Catholic men of letters; therefore, be it

"Resolved, That this Convention, in the name of the Catholic young men of the United States, offers him the tribute of its

Elizabeth N.J. May 5, 1885.

Your Grace

The encouragement and aid, which you have so generously accorded to my projected history of the Church, in response to the action of the Committee places under new and increased obligations

The sense of my inability to meet as I should desire the confidence placed in me, and the estimate formed of my ability, absolutely discourages me. I feel that I must produce a work that will justify my Patrons in the course they have adopted

To Your Grace in an especial manner, I consider my obligation extreme, as your name comes with all the historic weight of our most ancient See.

SHEA'S LETTER TO CARDINAL GIBBONS (1885)

Never have I seen so clearly that — I
must pray and work — ora et labora —
to attain the desired ends

Your Grace's
Most obd't Serv't in X
John Gilmary Shea

Most Rev James Gibbons DD
Archbishop of Baltimore

gratitude for the good he has done and the example he has given, and prays that his career of usefulness and honor may be prolonged yet many years; and

"Be it further resolved, That a certified copy of these resolutions be sent to Mr. Shea, in testimony of our admiration and respect."

Another interesting item belongs to this year. In his *History of the Diocese of Pittsburgh* (New York, 1880), Mgr. A. A. Lambing made use of De Courcy-Shea and of one of the *Relations* published by Dr. Shea without giving him any credit. The letter which he wrote on October 1, 1882, to Mgr. Lambing explains the matter:

"Now let me grumble a little. I was the first one to call attention to the fact that there were in Canada registers kept at French posts in this country, and when Mr. De Courcy was writing his sketches, we got through Hon. Jacques Viger lists of the missionaries at Ft. Duquesne, Ticonderoga, and other points. In writing up the diocese of Pittsburg we used this material. After a time Bishop O'Connor wrote to me to ask me to have the Fort Duquesne Register copied in Canada. I accordingly did so. After another interval in the course of our correspondence, he mentioned the interest I had excited, and the desire of many to copy it. I then offered to print it in my Cramoisy Series of tracts, limited to 100 copies and to give him 30 out the 100. He agreed to my proposal. I printed it, paid the bill and sent him the 30 copies, the 70 going to the subscribers to my series. Now a son of N. B. Craig had the assurance in a note to *Potter's Am. Monthly* to say that his father paid for the printing. He got a copy from me *gratis* and never paid a single cent of the cost of printing. It was printed by Mr. Munsell and I paid his bill, and Craig never paid nor offered to pay anything. He had nothing at all to do with it. In your volume (p. 34) you ignore me entirely and give the impression that Bishop O'Connor had it printed. I need not repeat that this is incorrect. The introduction that you cite was written by me. Subsequently when preparing another of my Cramoisy Series, comprising all the accounts I could gather of the battle of the Monongahela, I had considerable correspondence with the Beaujeu family, obtained a sketch of his life and his portrait which I engraved. In the course of it I found his name to be Lienard not Leonard. The official copyist at the prothonotary, some mere hack, had evidently blundered. At my request, the Rev. Felix Martin, S.J., compared the copy with the original, and the original register read clearly Lienard. In my tract *Relations Diverses,* I reprinted the entry correctly. The *Registre* as printed is not therefore absolutely to be depended on for the correctness of every word. Now you will admit that I have some reason to grumble. Protestants like Westcott give me credit, but others try to disparage and ignore me. Rev. Mr. Fitton copied thirty pages from me bodily and never mentions me; Rev. Mr. Horstmann takes an article of mine bodily and puts his own name to it. A miserable fellow like O'Kane Murray who never made a week's research, takes my book and rehashes it, and throws a slur on me. Even Mr. Lambing whom I respect, gives me no credit in the matter of the *Register* of Fort Duquesne, or in the supplementary charter, though it was I who called Mr. Cannon's atention to the errors and referred him to Westcott."

Two exceptional honors were conferred on Dr. Shea in the course of the year 1883. The first of these came in mid-Lent, when on Laetare Sunday, the University of Notre Dame singled Dr. Shea out as the most worthy Catholic layman in the United States for the honor of receiving the first Laetare Medal, which had just been instituted. The award was made towards the close of the year 1882, and in accepting the honor, Dr. Shea wrote to Father T. E. Walsh, C.S.C., then President of Notre Dame University:

"Believe me, as I open my letter with the warmest New Year's greetings for yourself and the noble College over which you preside, when I assure you that the holidays alone have given me courage to write.

"My first feeling was one of pride as an American Catholic that an American Catholic Institution should do so much for an American scholar.

"I do not think of myself, for I have never had an ambition, and any reputation I may have acquired is always tempered with

a kind of mild wonder as to its effect on my father had he lived
to see the estimate placed on one whom he persistently treated
as mentally inferior.

"My first feeling then was one of just pride in Notre Dame.
My feeling of personal gratitude came next, and here I fail
to find expression. The wish to make the close of my life a
peaceful and happy one with congenial minds, in daily intercourse, helping to give even in an humble way a true bent to
our young men on whose future so much depends, all this is
implied in your offer, and for nothing could I feel more deeply
or sincerely grateful. Accept my warmest thanks, and the thanks
of my family who feel it as sincerely as I do.

"But to accept the invitation, or to say that I am so situated
that I could not easily do so within a reasonable time, I am
still unprepared. The kind offer came so suddenly and unexpectedly. I am growing old and have never moved much. The
question requires prayer and consideration. I must pray your
indulgence for a time till I have weighed the question in all its
bearings, before I come to a decision, as I should never forgive
myself, if acting hastily I ever caused you to regret your noble
offer.

"If the spring opens favorably it will, perhaps, be wise for me
to make a pilgrimage to Notre Dame."

Dr. Shea's health did not permit him to make the journey to
Notre Dame, and the University deputed Maurice Francis Egan,
then with the *Freeman's Journal,* to go to Elizabeth and there
to confer the Medal upon him. The following address, prepared by Father Fitte, accompanied the Medal:

HOC
AD MAJOREM DEI O. M. GLORIAM
CATHOLICAE FIDEI AMPLIFICATIONEM
AC PRIMITIVAE AMERICAE FAMAM
D. JOANNI GILMARIAE SHEA
SCRIPTORI HISTORIAE FIDISSIMO
INDEFESSOQUE VERAE RELIGIONIS DEFENSORI
NOSTRAE DOMINAE UNIVERSITATIS
FACULTAS ET ALUMNI
AMICITIAE SEMPER MEMORES
PRECLARUMQUE INGENIUM MIRANTES
EXTRAORDINARIUM AURI NUMISMA
OFFERENDUM
UNANIMITER DECREVERUNT
A. D. 1883

Nos juvat hoc parvum claro transmittere donum
    Scriptori: summi pignus honoris erit.
Religio, pietas proavorum gloria libris
    Eminuere tuis, nostraque corda movent.
Gesta vales patrum semper narrare fidelis:
    Candida sincero scripta colore nitent.
Te sacrae fidei testem mirantur amici;
    Extollunt omnes laudibus ingenium.
Quum primos patriae tentas depingere mores,
    Simplex majestas grandis ubique micat.
Historiae fideique simul defensor haberis:
    Historicum nomen mundus uterque colit.
At mens alta solet famam superare silendo,
    Et virtus timido pectore magna latet.
Nostrum est ingenii velum removere modesti,
Praemiaque eximio solvere digna viro.

    Roma divinum Tiberim colebat;
    Nilus Aegypto sacer et decorum
    Maximus, Rhenusque pio coruscat
    Flumen honore.

Tu nostrum potius flumen venerabile dicis,
    Quod campis late dulcia dona ferat.
Tu rapidum fluvii mavis describere cursum,
    Tantaque de vasto munera nata sinu.
"O vitae flumen, regionis et ornamentum,"
    Exclamas "O Rex optime, magne Pater!
Salve, terra ferax, oculis ignota parentum:
    Europeae veteri jam novus orbis adest!

    Quam procul vidit moriens Columbus,
    Terra Gallorum genio patebis,
    Et feras gentes domuit supremo
    Numine Christus"!

Silvicolis coeli mysteria magna sacerdos
    Explicat, et Domini munera sacra docet,
Undique vana cadunt veterum simulacra decorum,

Servanturque pio pectore verba Dei.
Nunc "vestem nigram" tenero venerantur amore;
    Nunc Christi servos odia summa manent.
Ah! puro quoties rubuerant sanguine rivi
    Marytris ah! quoties sanguine silva madet!....

Jure quidem dignas volui persolvere grates:
    Multa enim libris sunt monumenta truis.
Hic occulis patriae et fidei observantur imago;
    Invenit hic pietas intermerata Deum,
Nec miror NOSTRAE DOMINAE te semper amicum:
    Virginis augustae diceris esse cliens.
Ne dubites alios Historiae praestare triumphos:
    Namque favet genio SANCTA MARIA tuo!

Dr. Shea replied in a letter and an illuminated address written in Latin:

TO THE FACULTY OF THE UNIVERSITY OF NOTRE DAME

"When a University, which holds the highest rank in the country, and has for more than a generation sent forth its trained Catholic alumni to take their part in the battle of life, decrees her Academic honors, it were rash to impeach her judgment. Yet when a Gold Medal, issued for the first time, was presented to me in your behalf with an address whose purely classic lines were animated by the highest gifts of poesy, the deep emotion that filled my soul could utter but the thought of my utter unworthiness of such a distinction. I could behold in myself no talent, learning or eminent service to religion and science that justified your choice. Love of the Church, love of my country, these indeed I have, and as I have labored animated by them, I receive with the deepest respect the honor you confer upon me, as a tribute to them.

"With deep gratitude and respect, I present to Notre Dame my sincere homage.

"JOHN GILMARY SHEA."

The accompanying address was expressed in elegant latinity, and printed upon parchment beautifully illuminated, with an elaborate arabesque and initial letter. These latter were painted in colors and gold by Dr. Shea's gifted daughter; and at the same time that the work manifested the artistic talent and execution of the young lady herself, it reflected great credit on the nuns who were her instructors. The whole was enclosed in an elegant framework of rough gold and maroon velvet. It reads as follows:

NOSTRAE DOMINAE UNIVERSITATIS FACULTATI ET ALUMNIS

Num donis me vultis, amici viventes, opprimere vestris,
Qui mortuos inter perdulci gradier amicos?
Ut quid relinquere charas vultis me cogere umbras,
In lucem actum, ac Magnum, invitum? Magnos habetis:
NEWTONUM habetis, et virum scientia factisque praeclarum,
Ac medicos inter est EMMET, qui celeber eminet certe,
Ecquid de CAROLO, legium perito, educam O'CONOR?
Post leges sunt bella,——ita! bellorum ac nobiles duces:
Nobilem ROSECRANS bene ornetis commeritis signis!
Vel etiam artis insigni, LAFARGIO, honorem donate,
Aut CORCORAN illi, theologo, digno merito, laude!
Nostrumque denique, qui dulciter canit ornate!
En viri! En magni! quos juxta, videte, quam tenuis ego!
Jam donum, amici, perenni manebit, pro monito mihi:
Quam longe ab eo consisto, quem me esse putastis.

JOANNES MARIAE SHEA.

The letter to the Faculty, and the address, were accompanied by a collection of the writings of the generous donor, and a copy of the Rheims Testament, with the following autograph letter:

"A copy of the rare original edition of the Catholic Testament translated by the learned Dr. Gregory Martin, alone, and printed at Rheims in 1582; two similar volumes containing the Old Testament were printed at Douay in 1609-10, forming what is known as the Douay Bible.

"As a translation, it is faithful and accurate: it is English of the best period, before the old traditional Catholic terms were forgotten.

"This volume is one to be looked upon with reverence. For generations it could be read in the British Isles only by stealth, as its possession was punishable with death."

To Father Thomas Walsh, the President, Dr. Shea wrote May 16, 1883:

"I have just forwarded to the University a box containing a reply to the elegant poetical address which was presented to me in your name by Mr. Egan.

"One in the daily turmoil of business life has little opportunity to woo the Muses and what my less polished lines lack in the exalted spirit of poetry and in harmony of numbers, will I trust be overlooked for the sake of the illumination in which my daughter's graceful hand has framed it. Nothing could exceed my surprise when Mr. Egan in the name of the University came to present the medal and the richly printed address.

"That I should be singled out for such an honor was entirely unexpected, for though my devotion to Holy Church has been absolute and true, it has not been my privilege to labor, as I would have desired, for her cause. What I have done is little, terribly little. Naming a few in different departments, on any of whom such an honor would have been well bestowed, I forebore to mention one to whom such a testimonial would be eminently due, Mr. McMaster, the oldest, the ablest of our Catholic editors, a man whose long service to the Catholic cause, felt throughout the land, entitle him to the highest place, though his severity of judgment and asperity of manner often prevent us from doing him full justice. In my case your personal friendship on the other hand has, V. Rev. Father, biased your better judgment. The generous and noble proposal already made filled me with concern and this new evidence of your friendship places me in the position of a helpless debtor, utterly unable to meet his enormous obligations. Accept for yourself and your venerable founder, as well as for the University over which you preside, the gratitude of my whole family by whom your name will ever be a cherished one."

On August 31, 1883, John W. Foster, the American Minister at Madrid, sent Dr. Shea the diploma creating him a corresponding member of the Real Academia de la Historia, an honor granted him on June 23 of that year.

The celebrated Letter of Pope Leo XIII to Cardinals De Luca, Pitra and Hergenroether, on *Historical Studies* (August

18, 1883) marks an important division in the history of Catholic historiography. In a young country like the United States it was but natural that the interest in its historic past should be fostered. Among the first to organize a movement towards a society for the study and writing of American Catholic history was Rt. Rev. A. A. Lambing, of the Diocese of Pittsburgh. After the little difficulty mentioned above had been cleared away between Mgr. Lambing and Shea, the latter spared no pains in assisting the Pittsburgh priest in his historical studies. Mgr. Lambing came to Elizabeth in the summer of 1883 and outlined a plan for the formation of an historical society. Guided by Dr. Shea he gathered a few friends around him on February 1, 1884, and organized the Ohio Valley Historical Society. In common with many others, Mgr. Lambing had long felt that too little interest was being manifested by American Catholics in collecting and preserving the records of the past. His plans included a Catholic historical magazine, and he began in July, 1884, the *Historical Researches in Western Pennsylvania principally Catholic.* In July, 1885, the periodical which had then reached its fifth number was changed to *Catholic Historical Researches.* The Ohio Valley Catholic Historical Society was not successful and disbanded after a few years. The *Researches* were purchased by Martin I. J. Griffin, of Philadelphia, and were conducted as a personal quarterly until his death in 1912, when they were merged into the quarterly *Records* of the American Catholic Historical Society of Philadelphia.

The Philadelphia Society was founded shortly after Monsignor Lambing's venture. A letter was sent out, dated July 4, 1884, to a chosen group of priests and laymen in the city, calling a meeting for the purpose on July 22.

Among those invited to assist in founding the American Catholic Historical Society was Dr. Shea, who replied on July 22, 1884:

"I received this morning as I was leaving for New York your invitation to attend the meeting today for the purpose of organizing a Catholic Historical Society.

"I regret that it was out of my power to join you, but I am sixty today, and feel that I am becoming a mummy or a fossil, an object for historians and palaeontologists to study out, rather than do any more studying or research myself.

"Your Society aims, I hope, more especially at local work; and there is really enough to be done in every state and almost in every diocese to call for a Catholic Historical Society in each one. The Pennsylvania Historical Society gives you encouragement, and I presume will give an alcove in its rooms for any collections you may form. This would insure their preservation, and be a great point. I suggest this because in my time I have seen collections dispersed and lost merely for want of a suitable place.

"Your endeavor has my heartiest wishes for its permanence and success, and with such experienced workers as Father Jordan, Father Middleton, and Mr. Griffin, the Society cannot fail to to give an impulse to investigation and save much precious knowledge from perishing. Too much has already gone.

"There must have been Registers, records, private letters journals, family records of Catholic priests and laymen which were lost because there was none to save them. Is it too late to collect and print the papers of Moylan, FitzSimons and Barry? Are there no journals of Catholic soldiers known besides that of my kinsman, McCurtin? The inscriptions on the grave stones in the old Catholic burial grounds down to, say, 1820, ought to be copied for preservation.

"Your Society will be the pioneer in the good work, and set an example for similar societies in other states. That I may live to see it lead to a general Society or Convention of local Societies, is my earnest wish.

"Expressing my hearty sympathy with your work, and looking forward hopefully to its future, I remain Rev. and dear Sirs, etc."

The organization of the Society was effected and support was immediately given by Archbishop Ryan and leading clergymen and laymen of the city. On August 13, 1884, Dr. Shea wrote to Monsignor Lambing: "They have started a Catholic Historical Society in Philadelphia, and I hope that it will succeed. There is certainly abundant material for them to work upon." After listing the many new aspects of the historical renaissance of 1884, Dr. Shea adds: "I never knew a greater interest to be felt or shown in the history of Notre Mère la Ste. Eglise Catholique, Apostolique, et Romaine in this part of world. This is extremely gratifying to me, and I trust we can encourage and maintain this feeling." In the earliest history of the Philadelphia Society we find the fact mentioned with considerable pleasure that Dr. John Gilmary Shea had written (December 10), asking to be enrolled as a member and informing the Philadelphia group that the United States Catholic Historical Society was about to be organized in New York City. The officers and trustees of the American Catholic Historical Society made an effort to induce the New York group to co-operate in such a way that one general orkanization for the country would be formed, but no decision was reached at the time and so both Societies have continued since 1884, as separate groups for the study of national Catholic history.

The founding of the United Catholic Historical Society was due to Dr. Shea's initiative. On October 31, 1884, Dr. Shea wrote to Archbishop Corrigan:

"Dr. Richard H. Clark and myself have long planned a Catholic Historical Society and we think the present a favorable opportunity. If we can obtain Your Grace's consent to preside at a meeting to be held in New York after the close of the Council, some of the Rt. Rev. Bishops known to take an interest would on their way home be able to attend, and clergymen and laymen of historic tastes could be invited. In this way the society would set out under the most favorable auspices as a society for the whole country. The meeting could be held in the vicinity of the Cathedral either at the house of the clergy or in some room in the Orphan Asylum, unless Your Grace suggests some other place."

Dr. Shea wrote on November 26, 1884, to Archbishop Leray, of New Orleans, to say that the first meeting of the proposed Society would be held "on a day to be fixed as soon as we know when the Council will close. We desire especially to be honored by your presence, if you intend to visit New York after the conclusion of your labors in Baltimore. In case this is not possible, will you not give the project your patronage and encouragement? We desire it especially, as Your Grace represents the

ARCHBISHOP M. A. CORRIGAN
NEW YORK

diocese of Louisiana, which when established in 1793 embraced all west of the Mississippi with Florida and the Gulfshore, and was in date second only to the See of Baltimore."

The first meeting was settled for December 9, and Dr. Shea wrote to Archbishop Corrigan: "In accordance with a suggestion of Rt. Rev. Bishop Ireland we fixed the first meeting of the Historical Society for Dec. 9th at 3 P. M. at the office of the Catholic Protectory, 715 Broome St. As Bishop Ireland is President of the Minnesota State Historical we wished his presence at the organization of ours. You will I fear be too much exhausted and fatigued to attend and preside at the meeting; that you may we all desire and solicit but we ask the influence of your name in case we are deprived of the honor of your presence. The project has received such encouragement that we begin to hope for success."

On his return from the Third Plenary Council of Baltimore, on December 8, 1884, Dr. Shea and Richard H. Clarke met a number of gentlemen interested in history at a meeting in the Catholic Protectory, in New York City, presided over by John Ireland. Shea, Clarke and Dr. Charles G. Herbermann were the leading spirits of the new Society. "We call our first meeting, as you see," he wrote to Martin I. J. Griffin, on December 2, 1884, "next week. This is, I hope, only the beginning, and similar Societies will arise in many parts, co-operating in the great work of rescuing our past from oblivion, and creating an interest in our noble history."

The second meeting took place on the seventeenth of the same month, and every effort was made by those present to induce Dr. Shea to accept the presidency. He persisted in declining, and Richard H. Clarke was chosen.

For the first two years (1884-1886) little was done, until a publication committee with Dr. Shea as its chairman, decided to issue a quarterly magazine. The first number appeared on January 1887, with the title *The United States Catholic Historical Magazine*. Four volumes were issued up to 1892. The purpose of the *Magazine*, as outlined by Dr. Shea, was "to present to the Catholics of the United States studies on points of the history of the Church by the scholars who were working in various parts of the country to tell the story of the early struggles of priest and

faithful, of heroic effort and often of heroic death. Little has
been hitherto done to save and preserve the documents, letters,
papers, and other material relating to the progress of Catholicity
in the United States."

Dr. Shea not only contributed some of his most valuable studies to the *Magazine* during its existence, but was its editor from
1887 to 1889. Shea was elected president of the Society in 1890.
After his death in 1892, interest in the work lagged, and from
1893 to 1897, it "slumbered in a state of coma." Dr. Herbermann became president in 1897, and the annual volumes *Historical Records and Studies* were begun in January, 1899. In the
first number Marc F. Vallette published a study on John Gilmary
Shea's life and works.

"To write a *History of the Church in the United States* has
been the hope and study of my life. The earlier frontier has
many unwritten chapters, and of some of these I have but
glimpses or faint clues, that may yet lead to fuller knowledge."
So Dr. Shea wrote in reply to Bishop Gilmour's encouragement
on April 20, 1882. Nevertheless, with all his diffidence over his
ability to master the appalling number of questions in American
Catholic history which no one had ever treated, he decided to
make a supreme effort toward the task, and through the years
1882-1883, along with the never-ending work connected with the
Frank Leslie publications of which he still remained editor-in-
chief, Dr. Shea began the first volume of his history, which he
called *The Catholic Church in Colonial Days the Thirteen Colonies—the Ottawa and Illinois Country—Louisiana—Florida—
Texas—New Mexico and Arizona.* The years to be covered by
this volume were 1521-1763.

His previous study of over forty years and all he had published
furnished him with first-hand material for this volume; and
yet he hesitated to begin upon the work of composition. To him
the study of the Church in this country was co-extensive with the
whole United States. At a dinner given to him in 1883, on the
occasion of the Laetare Medal, he said: "The work of Catholics is indelibly engraved on the map of America. Go to our
extreme boundary on the no.th of Maine. It is St. Mary's River.
Puritans and Yankees did not give that name. Go to our extreme
South, and in Florida we find St. Augustine and San Juan. No

one need be told who gave those names. So on the Pacific coast
we have San Francisco and Sacramento, Catholic names again.
In Virginia there was a colony of Dominican friars almost one
hundred years before Plymouth Rock was discovered."

Maurice Francis Egan writes of Dr. Shea at this time: "Dr.
Shea is of a cheerful, genial disposition, ever ready to oblige a
friend or stranger who may call on him for information, fond of
a joke, and possessed of a wealth of anecdote that makes him
excellent company. He is very happily married, and his two
daughters share in no small degree the talents of their father."
Once Dr. Shea made up his mind that his health and strength
would permit him to begin the work, it was upon his daughters
that he mostly relied to assist him in carrying it on successfully
to an end.

The first thing to do was to fill up whatever gaps there were
in his material. Few private libraries in the country were so
unique as was Dr. Shea's at this time. Among the twenty odd
thousand books, pamphlets, and manuscripts he had collected
were many of which he had the only known copy. But to complete the source-material at his hand, he began a correspondence
which included scholars of all countries. His letters to members
of the American hierarchy aroused a nation-wide interest, and
when the prelates met at the Third Plenary Council of Baltimore
in November-December, 1884, a committee, consisting of four
Archbishops (Gibbons, Williams, Corrigan and Ryan) was
appointed to co-operate with Dr. Shea in the publication of his
important work. In the few letters which passed between the
Committee and Dr. Shea that have been preserved, there are
two to Cardinal Gibbons which present interesting sidelights on
his preparation for the *History*. On May 22, 1884, Dr. Shea
writes to the Cardinal:

"Your Grace:-
"Mr. White, brother of the late Rev. Dr. White, called upon
me yesterday to ask about allowing Mr. Scharf, the historian,
the use of the letters and papers collected by Dr. White for his
projected history of our Church. As I recollect it, there is nothing written by Dr. White embodying the result of his long study
and it seems to me that the papers ought not to be placed in the

hands of one not likely to understand the affairs of the Church, and not known to be able to use them with discretion.

"There are certainly some papers that it would be injudicious to place where they could be employed mischievously. You will, I trust, pardon me, Your Grace, if I suggest that some one should go through them and make a list, selecting such as might be submitted to his examination. This will also give a memorandum to ensure their return. If there is no one who has the time or is familiar enough with the topics to do this, I will be happy to undertake it, in case the package is sent to me by express at my expense. I will examine them and return them.

"Mr. Murphy wishes me to prepare a volume containing a life and some of the pastorals and other writings of Archbishop Carroll. I feel that it ought to be done and would cheerfully undertake it, but he wishes to issue it before the Plenary Council meets in October. This gives me too brief a time. If he will defer the publication, and I have Your Grace's approval and can obtain access to any diaries he may have kept or other documents in the archives of the See, I shall agree to do my best.

"I have forwarded by express a copy of *Catholic Address to Washington* which I printed privately some years ago.

"Asking for myself and mine Your Grace's blessing, I remain,
"*Your most obdt. Sevt. in Xt*
"JOHN GILMARY SHEA."

In the April and July (1884) issues of the *American Catholic Quarterly Review,* Dr. Shea had written two articles on the Councils of Baltimore which attracted considerable attention from the prelates who were to meet in that city in November for the Third Plenary Council. Many letters were sent to Dr. Shea as a consequence, and among them was one from Cardinal Gibbons asking him to draft out a page of statistics for the problem of loss and gain which would undoubtedly be discussed in the Council. Dr. Shea replied from Schooley's Mountain, N. J., on August 10, 1884:

"*Your Grace:*
"I must apologize for my delay in replying to Your Grace's letter of the 1st. A telegram from Mgr. Seton reached by house in Elizabeth on the 2d, a few hours after a hurried visit I had

paid to it, for I have been taking a vacation for the first time in many years.

"The telegram reached me some days later, but Your Grace's letter only came to my hands yesterday at my house. I selected the Almanacs for several years preceding and following 1866 and notes of population. I made up an approximate estimate for 1865 taking each diocese according to the rate of progress shown these estimates gave a total of 3,939,500.

"A similar calculation for 1866 gave 4,356,000.

"I think therefore that in that year the population was rather over than under four millions. The estimate for New York and Brooklyn has, I am satisfied, been too high for many years, that of Bishop Dubois in 1829 was evidently so.

"There was a rashness in a layman like myself attempting to write on the Councils held in this country, and no one feels his imperfections more sensibly than I do; but I wrote with the view of so depicting the progress and the glory of the Church as to give the younger men who are growing up a sense of pride in corresponding to the grace of faith which they received in baptism. That my efforts can elect from Your Grace such words of approval gives me the consolation that my articles are not deemed presumptuous but calculated to do good.

"The Plenary Council of 1884 will undoubtedly be the last held in my life time and I am anxious to witness some of the public Sessions. I hope to benefit by the strength I am gaining to visit the Catholic Capital of the United States in November to gratify this wish.

"With the deepest veneration and respect

"Your Grace's most obedient servt. in Xt.,

"JOHN GILMARY SHEA."

It was while he was in Baltimore atending the closing public sessions of the Council that the group of prelates already mentioned asked him to meet them for the purpose of discussing a complete history of the Church in this country. The first centenary of the establishment of the See of Baltimore was close at hand (1889) and it was believed by all that the time was propitious for a scholarly review of the hundred years that had passed.

What had been written and published was unsatisfactory. On that all were agreed. Even the De Courcy-Shea *History* which Dr. Shea had brought up to date when he re-issued it in 1879, was but a partial glimpse into the advance made by Catholicism in the United States from Carroll's day to that time. The other *Histories* which had been published by McGee (1855); White (1868); and O'Kane Murray (1876), were popular presentations of Church progress, largely written with an eye upon the political and religious problems of the Irish race. What was needed was a thorough study of all the conditions in which the vigorous young Church of America found itself during its first century of national life, and an impartial narrative of the hindrances, both within and without the fold, to its progress.

John Gilmary Shea had never, in all his long career of forty years in the field of American Catholic history, blinked at the truth. He had never hidden the undesirable facts of our history under platitudes or specious appeals to racial pride. He was trusted by the bishops as probably no other layman before or since his day.

On his return from the Council, it was with the assurance that he would be supported in his work, and he saw in prospect the fulfilment of his life's dream. By March 1, 1885, he was ready to announce the *History* and was able to promise that the volumes would be issued at intervals, the first to appear on May 1, 1886, and the last in not more than five years (May 1, 1890).

His earliest outline included five volumes. The *"History,"* he writes, in March, 1885, "as I have planned it, will form five large volumes, to be illustrated, as far as may be, with portraits, facsimiles, representations of early churches, historic sites, relics, etc.; each volume to be complete and independent in itself, with a distinct title and index, but the whole series forming a consecutive and complete narrative——

    I.　*The Colonial Church under Spanish, French, and English Flags.*

    II.　*Archbishop Carroll and the Establishment of the Hierarchy.*

    III.　*The Church in the Atlantic States.*

    IV.　*The Church in the Valley of the Mississippi.*

    V.　*The Church on the Pacific Coast.*

An appeal was sent out for subscriptions in March 1885, with the following announcement:

"Most of the leisure hours of my life and much of my means have been devoted to studies, as well as to the acquisition of every book, periodical, paper, and document, whose existence I could trace, bearing on the early and actual history of the Church in this country, the efforts of the pioneer Catholics and their clergy, the Indian missions, the organization of the Church under English, French, and Spanish rule, the religious life and discipline that grew up, the vicissitudes of the Church and its ultimate steady development to its present condition.

"It has been the purpose of my life to write this history, hoping that the evening of my days would give me the means and leisure to accomplish the task. Little fitted by studious habits for active business life, I have maintained myself by literary labor comfortably, but no more; and year by year my leisure has been required by work needed for my support, so that a competence on which to retire is now out of the question.

"This disappointment I accept without repining and without a murmur.

"Recently some of the Most Rev. Archbishops and Right Rev. Bishops, with several of the Clergy, have, unexpectedly to me, taken the matter into consideration, regarding it as important for the Church in this country that the knowledge of the subject acquired by so many years of study should be published and made accessible; they have debated on the best means of securing me the necessary leisure, and of completing my collections, where printed or manuscript matter becomes accessible."

There was no lack of encouragement. Cardinal Gibbons was a constant source of support to the venerable historian, and the letters which passed between them, almost up to the day of Dr. Shea's death, are a glimpse into a little known side of James Gibbons' character.

Dr. Shea wrote on May 1, 1885: "The encouragement and aid which you have so generously accorded to my projected History of the Church in response to the action of the Committee places me under new and increased obligations. The sense of my inability to meet as I should desire the confidence placed in me, and the estimate formed of my ability, absolutely discourages me.

I feel that I must produce a work that will justify my Patrons in the course they have adopted. To Your Grace in an especial manner, I consider my obligation extreme, as your name comes with all the historic weight of our most ancient See. Never have I seen so clearly that I must pray and work—*ora et labora*—to attain the desired end."

Second only to Cardinal Gibbons was the support of Archbishop Corrigan of New York. Michael Augustine Corrigan had been coadjutor-Archbishop of New York from 1880 until the death of Cardinal McCloskey on October 10, 1885. Around Archbishop Corrigan was a small group of priests whose interest in Dr. Shea's project was as keen as his own. Among these were: Monsignors Quinn, Preston, and Edwards of New York; Father John M. Farley, who succeeded Dr. Corrigan in 1902 and became the second Cardinal of New York in 1911; Rev. Patrick Corrigan of Hoboken; and Messrs. Eugene Kelly, William R. Grace, and many others. Interest was not confined to New York, however, but if any one among all those who have been or might be mentioned, deserves to be honored as Dr. Shea's most generous and most intelligent adviser and supporter, it is Archbishop Corrigan. Few members of the American hierarchy of the day possessed his wide knowledge of the inner history of the Church in the United States; and it was Dr. Corrigan's great patience, and patience, indeed, was necessary with a scholar embarking on so broad an expanse as the history of the Catholic Church in the United States from 1492 to the then present, that carried the work of Shea to completion and to success.

Dr. Shea wrote to his Maecenas on May 1, 1895:

"I called to thank you in person for the interest Your Grace has taken in the project to enable me to devote myself to writing the *History of the Church*. But for Your Grace's direction and influence little I am certain would have been effected but with it all difficulties seemed to vanish.

"The confidence felt in me and the result that you and the kind patrons, who, led by Your Grace's influence, have co-operated, may justly expect at my hands, have completely discouraged me now that I am brought face to face with the task. The last week has been one of the most miserable of my life so easily am I depressed. I have set to work studying up the whole field to learn first what the great deficiencies of material are and where to look for the information to supply them. Sabin's *Dictionary of Books relating to America* with nearly 100,000 titles and the Catalogues of all great libraries will be thoroughly examined that nothing in print may escape me. Collections of documents in public and private depositories are less easily reached but many will be accessible. For those in the archives of dioceses which formerly had jurisdiction over parts of this country I need a letter to the present Archbishop or Bishop. Enclosed is a facsimile of a hand that you recognize, my warm and kind friend Archbishop Bayley. That letter opened to me many avenues of research. If a similar letter of introduction in the name of His Eminence signed by Your Grace, also by the Most Rev. Archbishop of Baltimore, can be drawn up in which it would appear that I am now at work under the direct sanction of such members of our Hierarchy, I would reproduce it and feel assured that every facility will be afforded me."

On June 20, 1885, he wrote to Cardinal Gibbons:

"In my work on the *History* which I have undertaken, I have arranged all my material for the colonial part and sketched out the narrative, and I have done the same for the *Life and Times of Archbishop Carroll,* but of course less fully. The late Archbishop Bayley informed me that there was a considerable collection of documents relating to the early Jesuit missions in Maryland which had remained there from the times of Archbishop Carroll. From other sources where incidental mention was made of them, I infer that they contain much that will be of great importance for my work, in order to correct and enlarge my sketch. For the life of Archbishop Carroll himself the material in Your Grace's archives is the main source. It is therefore to ask Your Grace most respectfully when it will be convenient for me to examine the earlier documents that I may arrange to visit Baltimore and spend some time at the work.

"There are many points also in regard to which I desire guidance in order to avoid giving ground for reviving vexed questions and confining myself to statements that cannot be disputed."

How thoroughly Dr. Shea examined the Baltimore Cathedral

Archives is well-known to all who have worked among these precious papers of our Catholic past. Dr. Shea brought to the work of research a knowledge of American Catholic history which no other scholar has ever possessed, and his notes and comments sometimes on separate sheets of paper, sometimes on the back of the document itself, have often proved invaluable for later students in the same field.

The period of discovery and colonization (1492-1690) he had thoroughly covered in his *Catholic Missions* and in his translation of De Courcy. The colonial period of provincial America and the struggle for the Mississippi Valley (1690-1763) had been equally mastered. The hazy epoch of our Revolution and the faint beginnings of Catholic organization after the Treaty of Paris (1763-1784) were still to be cleared up with documentary material. The national period, or the period of the Church in this country under an established hierarchy, from Carroll's acceptance of the Prefecture-Apostolic in 1785 to his own day, Shea knew in broad and concise outlines. But for all these epochs, he needed documents and more documents.

Archbishop Corrigan and his Secretary, the future Bishop of Brooklyn, Dr. Charles E. McDonnell, used their influence to open to Dr. Shea the closed Archives of the Sacred Congregation of Propaganda Fide. Brother Henry Foley, who wrote on November 5, 1885, that "in my present state, you must consider me as a dead man," had handed over his request for documents from the Stonyhurst Archives, to Father John Morris, S. J., and to a young scholastic, who was later to become one of England's from the Stonyhurst Archives to Father John Morris, S. J. Lord Arundel of Wardour wrote, in an almost undecipherable script, valuable notes on the Baltimore family and on the early projects of English Catholic colonization in the New World. Richard R. Elliott was indefatigable in searching out data for the history of the French in and around Detroit. Archbishop Leray, of New Orleans, was unsparing in his efforts to bring light into the confusing story of the rise of the Diocese of New Orleans. The members of the Society of Jesus, to which John Gilmary Shea had once belonged, were generous in allowing him access to their private archives, in order that nothing should escape his notice. The Loretto Sisters of Kentucky, the Daughters of Charity of

Cincinnati, and the Ursulines of Brown County, Ohio, sent him papers and periodicals, without which he could not have penned his story of the Church in the Middle West.

If ever, in the history of history-writing in the United States, a scholar held a nation-wide interest in his work, that scholar was John Gilmary Shea. Financially, he was to lose rather than to gain by the publication of the five volumes of his *History,* but in ways that could not be measured by money, he awakened in the hearts of Catholic priests and laymen all over the land an interest in our Catholic past which has lasted till our own day and has been the source of inspiration to thousands since his death.

To Doctor Charles E. McDonnell, Dr. Shea wrote on September 17, 1885, asking him to facilitate further investigations in the Propaganda Archives. William Maziere Brady, who had included some important documents on America in his *Episcopal Succession in England, Scotland and Ireland* (1876), and upon whom Dr. Shea depended to direct the search at Propaganda, had left for Australia with Cardinal Moran. In the emergency, Doctor McDonnell's acquaintance with the Roman officials proved valuable and Dr. Shea was able to secure the documents he needed.

On September 21, 1885, Dr. Shea wrote to Archbishop Corrigan:

"How can I thank you for your kindness in again addressing the Secretary of the Propaganda. Mr. Maziere Brady had access to documents giving some light on our Maryland Missions and I hoped to obtain from him more information than he printed. The connection of events seemed so probable that I could not refrain from asking to see whether the papers examined by Mr. Brady did not contain more. From England, though I fail to obtain any details as to the Franciscans, information comes very unexpected to me in regard to projects of Catholic colonization before Lord Baltimore and there is every reason to believe that the famous voyage of Sir Humphrey Gilbert in Queen Elizabeth's reign is connected with a Catholic project, and that a plan formed at a later day was defeated by the famous Jesuit Father Persons, although supported by the brave Lord Arundel of Wardour.

That the early Franciscan Mission in Maryland is not altogether imaginary is proved by two facts recently elicited, one, that in 1712, and some years before, Lord Baltimore allowed them 1000 lbs. of tobacco a year, and the other that a library in Maryland has two books bearing the name. It must not be supposed that Father Haddoc was such a smoker that he required an allowance of three pounds a day; in justice to the old missionary I will add that all values in Maryland were then estimated in tobacco. The Minister of the established Church received from every person Catholic as well as Protestants 40 lbs. of tobacco every year. There are complaints extant from these worthy gentlemen that, as the law did not fix the quality to be delivered, most that came to their hands was very bad. I do not suppose that a Catholic so taxed would pick out the best of his stock of tobacco to pay so unjust a tax."

Again on November 19, 1885, Dr. Shea writes:

"With the most sincere feelings of regard and respect I congratulate you on your succession to the see of New York, to which notwithstanding my long residence in New Jersy I feel a native allegiance. No one can more earnestly wish you a long administration full of consolation to yourself and profit to all.

"As an offering of my fealty in the future and a mark of gratitude for the past I have taken the liberty of forwarding to Your Grace some of my historic contributions of which I beg your acceptance.

"By your kindness I heard with deep interest your sermon at the Month's Mind of his late Eminence. The striking virtue which characterized him, his singular prudence, had impressed me deeply, although I did not know some facts stated by Your Grace; but they called up to my mind two books of P. S. Casserly, one denouncing Dr. Pise with all the violence that marked that learned man and practical Catholic, the other his translation of Thomas à Kempis' *Garden of Roses* with a dedication to Rev. John McCloskey.

"In a visit to Philadelphia I went carefully through Father Farmer's registers, and have since studied carefully the route of his visits to New Jersey in regard to which there had been more conjecture than research. With old maps and books I think that

I can trace every visit accurately. There is absolutely no proof whatever that he ever visited New York before the Revolution. At Quebec, I discovered two curious facts which can probably be made clear by documents in the Propaganda. One is that after La Salle descended the Mississippi river with the Recollect Fathers, as detailed in Le Clercq, application was made and supported by Louis XIV to have Vicariates-Apostolic established in the Mississippi Valley, and that the Pope actually did erect them. When Bishop St. Vallier of Quebec learned of this, he protested against the dismemberment of his diocese, declaring that the Mississippi had been discovered by Father Marquette, a priest of his diocese, and Louis Joliet, a pupil of his seminary. Louis XIV had appointed a committee consisting of some French Bishop and his confessor Père La Chaise who reported in favor of the Bishop of Quebec and the Pope then suppressed the Vicariates.

"The document unfortunately gives no dates, and does not name the Vicariates or those appointed, whom I suspect to have been Recollects. The other fact is that after the Conquest of Canada, a request was forwarded to Rome by some one asking that the Bishop of Quebec be empowered to administer confirmation in Maryland and Pennsylvania. I found a letter of the Cardinal-Prefect to Bishop Briand in regard to the matter, and it is the first act I have ever seen or heard of showing any direct attention of the Propaganda to the affairs of these colonies, although doubtless they were treated incidentally in connexion with the English mission. The Jesuit Father George Hunter visited Canada soon after the Conquest and the representation to Rome may have arisen from some report made by him. If I have not taxed your kindness and condecension beyond all tolerance I make a note of what might be looked for at the Propaganda. Both points will be evidence of the control of the missions in this country by the Propaganda, which may hereafter be valuable."

Another letter, dated December 1, 1885, to Archbishop Leray of New Orleans, shows how the first volume of the *History* was proceeding:

"In compliance with the wish of several Archbishops and Bishops and encouraged by the subscription made in advance I have been working in earnest at the *History of the Church* in this country most of this year. The first volume includes all down to 1783. For the part in the English colonies I have collected all material that I can trace and most of the narrative is written. For the Spanish part I have most encouraging success for Florida, Texas, and New Mexico. The French part touches Maine, and of which I have much, some hitherto unknown. For the Mission in New York I have also abundant material. For Michigan, Wisconsin and Illinois my documents are also rich. But for Louisiana, I now appeal to Your Grace. My first published work in 1853 was on the *Discovery of the Mississippi* by Father Marquette followed by the Recollect Fathers under La Salle. I have Iberville's Voyage, in which he was accompanied by a Recollect and Jesuit. Some years ago I printed letters from Messrs. Montigny and his associates, sent out from the Seminary of Quebec by St. Vallier, with his Lordship's act founding the Mission.

"I have Abp. Taschereau's history of that Mission which finally centered at Tamarois in Illinois. This includes the very curious history of Rev. M. Le Maire's coming to Louisiana.

"I have recently discovered a protest of Bp. St. Vallier against the action of the Pope who erected some Vicariates-Apostolic in the Mississippi Valley, which on his protest were suppressed. Investigation is now in progress at Rome to find all about this. For the Jesuit Mission there are letters in the *Lettres Edifiantes,* the *Bannissement des Jesuites de la Louisiane* and a few letters recently found. My great want is documents to give anything like a connected sketch of the history of the Church among the settlers of Louisiana while the Capuchin Fathers were in control. There is nothing in the Archives at Quebec either in the Archévêché or the Seminary. Will Your Grace permit your Rev. Secretary to inform me what the archives of your See can supply? 1. Are there any reports, sketches or statements made by Capuchins between 1725 and 1783? 2. Are there any documents by Rt. Rev. Cyril de Barcelona, Bishop of Tricali, who, as auxiliary Bishop, administered that portion of the diocese of Cuba and, after its division, of St. Christopher of Havana from 1776 to 1793? 3. At what date do the oldest Registers begin and are they perfect from the beginning? 4. Is the Bull erecting the

Diocese of Louisiana and the Floridas (1773) preserved in the archives? 5. Which are the oldest parishes outside New Orleans and which of them have ancient Registers?

"If your Grace will permit your Rev. Secretary to have an examination made I will meet all expense: and I can then know what material I can hope to obtain for my work. I wish to make it full and faithful for every part of the country: and feeling that my material is not complete for Louisiana, I beg Your Grace's favor and indulgence."

The daily journeys from Elizabeth to New York were used in collating all the source-material which had arrived, and, every available moment that could be spared from his duties as editor was used to compose the rough outline of the work on which he was engaged. After his return to his home in the evening, a short time was given to his family and then the long hours of writing were begun. About midnight one of his daughters would persuade him to take a small repast, and after that he was left to work, sometimes until the dawn appeared. Fortunately, Mrs. Shea was an excellent manager, for her husband never could understand domestic affairs. All in all the situation was ideal for a scholar who was practically absorbed in his work.

CHAPTER VII

The "History of the Catholic Church in the United States"

1886-1892)

By November, 1886, the first volume of the *History* was in type and was eagerly watched for by the patrons of the work as well as by all who were interested in Catholic American history. "The work which I have endeavored to do carefully and conscientiously," Shea writes in the preface of this volume, "has cost me more labor and anxiety than any book I ever wrote; it has caused me not seldom to regret that I had undertaken a task of such magnitude. To my fellow-students of American history, from whom I have for so many long years received encouragement, sympathy, and aid, I submit my work with some confidence, trusting to their past courtesy and kindness. From those of my own faith I ask forbearance, hoping that the volume may prove of some service till a writer with a clearer head for research, more patience in acquiring the necessary books and documents, and greater knowledge and skill in presenting the results affords the Catholics of the United States a book adequate to the subject."

The first volume was issued under the title *The Catholic Church in the Colonial Days* (1521-1763), and is divided into four books, each of which is again divided into three parts: the Catholic Church in the (a) English, (b) Spanish, (c) French colonies or territories. In reality the volume is made up of three sections, devoted to the three chief colonizing nations, England, Spain and France, with two chronological divisions common to the three sections: 1500-1690; 1690-1763. A certain amount of confusion arises from the plan followed by Dr. Shea; but it was, and still is, the only logical method of treating in a general fashion so large a subject.

On its appearance, the welcome it received removed all doubts from Dr. Shea's mind. It was recognized as a splendid achievement; and in the hearts of all his friends there was but one thought, one prayer, namely, that Dr. Shea might be spared to complete the great task he had begun.

Two years were to pass, crowded with many anxieties, financial and family troubles, and his own fitful spells of exhaustion, before the second volume, *The Life and Times of Archbishop Carroll,* was ready for the press. To Monsignor (Cardinal) Farley, he wrote on October 18, 1888:

"Rt. Rev. Dear Friend:

"The Life and Times of Archbishop Carroll is, as you know, ready; and it has cost me great labor, absorbing all my leisure and impairing my health seriously. It covers an important period, and really the history of the Church during it has not hitherto been known. Not only are errors and misrepresentations corrected, but whole chapters are new contributions.

"I have made the volume so large and expensive, that I am in considerable debt: and I see no way except to have another appeal for patrons of the work. There have been eight deaths, and there were when I issued the volume eight delinquents, some of whom wish to withdraw altogether.

"By making up a list of 250 prominent Catholics in the United States, it seems to me that 25 or 30 new patrons ought to be secured. With that number I can complete the work without anxiety.

"With many thanks for all your kindness in the matter I remain

"Your deeply obliged friend and servt.,
"John Gilmary Shea."

Among those upon whose assistance Dr. Shea particularly depended for his *Carroll* was the late Father E. I. Devitt, S. J., then at Woodstock College. Dr. Shea wrote on April 16, 1888, to the Jesuit historian:

"I have been hoping to get down to Woodstock, but see no immediate prospect of paying you a visit. I am closing up the *Life of Archbishop Carroll* and have some difficulties. I can find no facts about the opening of Georgetown College in 1791 or anything about it till the characteristic display made by Rev. M. Du Bourg when he retired. I hoped to find something in Father Summer's articles, but after giving the Proposals he bounds over to Du Bourg's resignation. I could not find any letters at Baltimore addressed to Bp. Carroll in regard to the College or its progress. In his letter to his friends I find only passing allusions generally showing that the management did not act in conformity with his ideas and referring to its want of success.

"Of Rev. Mr. Plunkett I find no letters, reports, circulars.

"Can you help me to any facts in regard to the College before its incorporation or indeed before Father Grassi gave it new life? I am equally in the dark as to the foundation of Holy Trinity Ch., Georgetown, and cannot find when or by whom it was begun.

"As to the first Church in Washington City I have only a few vague notes.

"In the process of Abp. Marechal against the Maryland mission I find he refers to some brief of 1789 as giving the Bishop of Baltimore control. I know no brief but that erecting the See of Baltimore that gives the Bishop the right to administer ecclesiastical revenue, but I cannot believe he rested his claim on that. Do you know any brief of 1789 referring to the property of Maryland? You once kindly informed me that there were several books in Woodstock Library printed in this country before 1820 which Finotti had not included. I enclose a list of the earlier ones known to me, and if you can add other titles I shall feel grateful. In the list those with x I have in my collection. As Spring gets on I do hope to pay you a visit."

On October 1, 1888, Dr. Shea sent out to his patrons a printed announcement, stating that "owing to protracted ill-health, the second volume of my *History of the Catholic Church in the United States,* embracing the *Life and Times of Archbishop Carroll* has been delayed till the present time." That same week, he wrote to Cardinal Gibbons:

"My health since Spring has been such that work on my history has been almost impossible. At last, however, I am relieved by seeing the *Life and Times of Archbishop Carroll* sent off to Your Eminence and others who have kindly patronized the undertaking. With much hitherto unpublished documents regarding him and his acts personally, I have blended the history of the Church in the country to 1815, and I trust have added much. There were subjects that required care, but I endeavor to give facts plainly, leaving them to act as warnings, and avoiding as far as possible any judgments that will excite discussion.

"There are many curious points: the French intrigue to put the Catholics here under a Bishop in France; Bp. Burke's project of a Vicariate-Apostolic in the Northwest; the Prefecture Apostolic of Scioto; and the absurd proposal of a Bishop at Oneida. The mission work of the Sulpitians is at last told with some detail and it was needed, for many seemed to think they never did anything except conduct the seminary at Baltimore.

"I hope that the volume will by your approval justify the encouragement which Your Eminence has given me."

Cardinal Gibbons again came generously to his aid in order that no delay should prevent the appearance of the third volume. In thanking His Eminence (October 10, 1888), Dr. Shea said: "I hope that your impression of my *Life of Abp. Carroll* will equal your favorable anticipation. The state of the Church in the whole country, the difficulties which retarded its progress, and Carroll's great work in harmonizing, stimulating, and accomplishing much with the feeblest resources, will be better known, and the labors of the pioneer priests, though many left no record but a name, will be better understood."

To Father Patrick Corrigan, who was a constant source of encouragement, he wrote on October 15, 1888: "After a protracted period of ill-health caused by overwork I am able to send out the second volume of my *History*. It will enlighten many as to our early struggles. My researches throw light on several points: Bp. Challoner's efforts to give us a Bishop; the Catholic Chaplains in the Continental Army; England's failure to raise a Catholic regiment here; Bancroft's libels; the French intrigues to subject the Church here to a Court Bishop in France; the indictment and trial of Rev. J. Cheverus in Maine."

The second volume of his *History* was even more successful than the first. The times were almost within the memory of many who were still living. By that period, on account of the many assemblies of the bishops at Baltimore between 1829 and 1884, the figure of John Carroll loomed up in the Catholic life of the United States as did that of George Washington in its political history. John Carroll had stood, as Dr. Shea wrote at the time, "as a noble and central figure for nearly thirty years (1785-1815) of that half-century as the controlling and guiding mind in the affairs of the Church." To all the friends who had aided him thus far in his researches, he now added the revered name of Father A. L. Magnien, then Superior of the Sulpicians in this country, and that of a brilliant newcomer in the field, Professor James

Farnham Edwards, of Notre Dame University, to whom we owe the valuable collection known as the Catholic Archives of America, now housed in that institution.

The *Life of John Carroll* runs along more smoothly than the first volume, since there is no break in the chronology. There is a charm about the style and a warmth to the pages that disclose how near its author had come to the heart of the Father of the American hierarchy. Dr. Shea had one keen regret at this time: that he had not begun to write our Catholic history earlier in life. "Attempting now to write history," he says, "I regret often and bitterly that I did not begin in boyhood to do what you have done so well. I knew some of the little body who began the first Catholic congregation in New York City, and might have filled notebooks with details."

Before the end of the year 1889, Dr. Shea had accepted the editorship of the *Catholic News,* of New York City, and in this post, week-by-week, he filled its editorial page with so many historical facts, gathered in the course of a life-time of study, that this weekly journal must be given a place of first importance in the source-material of that part of Catholic history which Dr. Shea did not treat.

One of these editorials (June 8, 1890), should be known by every child in our Catholic schools. It is entitled: *Sources of the Catholic History of the Country:*

"The Catholic history of the country begins with the earliest explorers by sea and land. For many years these were all Catholic: Cabot, Verrazzano, Gomez, Ponce de Leon, Pineda on the coast; Cabeza de Vaca, Father Mark of Nice, Coronado in the interior, were all Catholics. All bore with them their Catholic Faith and the services of the Catholic Church. Our first chapter is to be sought in the record of these expeditions. Here we can trace the Catholic names given to points on the coast from Ste. Croix, or Holy Cross River, to Corpus Christi. When settlements were attempted, the first were made by Catholics. Ponce de Leon in Florida, Ayllon on the James River in Virginia, Tristan de Luna at Pensacola, Menendez at St. Augustine, Oñate at Santa Fé, Champlain at Neutral Island. All were Catholic and their history is to be traced in the Spanish annalists like Barcía, in the history of religious orders, in documents in the Spanish archives, in the works of Champlain, the Relations of New Mexico. Is all mention of these settlements excluded from general histories of the United States and even State histories from ignorance or prejudice? Why do they suppress all mention of them? If Catholics try to bring forward some real true history they are denounced. Evidently some people love ignorance better than knowledge.

"When English settlements were made on the coast Catholics settled in Maryland. Their history is a noble one, but how, of late years, men have strained their ingenuity to falsify it! There is not a baser chapter in American literature than the malignant efforts to decry the Calverts and the early Maryland Catholics and deprive them of their just glory. Before 1829 not a syllable was uttered, but when Catholic emancipation was extorted in England, Protestants began to try to show that Protestantism had always been the very pink of toleration, and to consign the penal laws to oblivion. The real history of early Maryland is to be read in the Relations, in Father White's *Narratio,* in the Foley Documents, and in the terrible penal laws which cannot be blotted out of the statute book, in the published Archives, and in unpublished documents. The laws of Massachusetts, Rhode Island, Connecticut, Virginia, the Carolinas and Georgia show the infamous penal laws of those colonies, the war on Catholic education, industry, civil rights and, we might almost say, existence. To the North, West and South we trace Catholic progress in the Jesuit Relations, the Narrative of Marquette, of La Salle and his companions, Membré and Hennepin, in brave Iberville and stout Penecaut, in the printed works of Dumont, Le Page du Pratz, Bernard de la Harpe; in works on New Mexico, Benavides, Lopez, Salmeron, Morfi, Siguenza, in Palou's *Life of Serra* and his larger narrative, in the lives of venerable Anthony Margil and in unpublished documents. Later still, when the Catholics of the country were placed under a single head and a single organization, the works of Catholic priests and Catholic laymen are to be sought in hundreds of sources, and depositories too many to enumerate in an article.

"Now, what history of the United States used in schools shows even inadequately the progress of the Catholic element from the earliest days to its present attitude, when one-sixth of the whole population belongs to it? In the books used in the Protestant

Public Schools, the Catholic element is studiously ignored or maliciously misrepresented. More space is given to the religion of the Separatists and Puritans of New England, misrepresented to suit the times, than is even given to the Catholic, in the whole country, for a period extending from 1813 to 1890, and geographically extending from the whole Atlantic seaboard to the shores washed by the Pacific. Poet and artist seek inspiration in Catholic annals, but they are studiously ignored by those who profess to give history. History!"

The work on the third volume, which was to carry the story of the Church from 1815 to 1844, went on side-by-side with the examination of the proofs of *Carroll.* The New Year, 1889, brought him another unique honor. He had rescued from what was practically oblivion hundreds of facts which enhanced the renown of John Carroll among Americans generally, and among these facts was Carroll's part, as principal, in the founding of Georgetown College. The centenary of this venerable school came that year, and early in January, Dr. Shea received a letter from Father J. Havens Richards, S. J., then President of Georgetown University, telling him that the authorities had decided to confer upon him a medal in honor of his *Life of Archbishop Carroll* and suggesting that he write a centenary *History of Georgetown College.* Father Richards wrote:

"I have the honor of announcing to you that it is the desire of our Faculty to confer upon you, at our coming Centennial celebration, the degree of Doctor of Laws. We are aware that this distinction has already been bestowed upon you by another institution, but we wish to add the approbation of our University to this testimony of your learning and the immense value of your historical and linguistic labors. For this purpose, no time would seem more appropriate than the occasion on which we are to celebrate the first Century of Catholic higher education in the United States, a period on which your pen has shed so much light.

"It is our intention also to recognize the merit of your last work on the 'Life and Times of Archbishop Carroll' and its connection with the founding of our own University, by striking a gold medal, to be presented to yourself on the day of the Academic Session, February 22, 1889, which is the third day of the Centennial exercises. If it pleases you to accept this testimony of our esteem and gratitude, I should like you to have taken immediately, at our expense, by some good photographer, several photographs of yourself, (bust only), from different positions, say front, profile, three quarters, etc. Especial care must be taken that the photographer do not tamper in any way with the lines of the negative so taken. They usually obliterate all the fine and characteristic lines of the face on the pretence of beautifying it. If the 'Laetare' medal awarded you some years ago by the University of Notre Dame has a medallion portrait upon it, we should be pleased to see it also.

"I trust that you will pardon my entering into these details. My excuse is the close proximity of the celebration, which will render the promptest action necessary."

In reply, Dr. Shea said:

"I have been laid up since the 2nd with a broken knee pan, ruptured ligaments, and bruises, the result of a fall stepping from an ill-constructed elevator in New York.

"Your letter reached me only last evening. I have been greatly interested in the coming Centenary of Georgetown University, though Providence did not guide me to its walls for stores of learning.

"Though a pretty hard student through life, I left school at 13, and academic honors always seem to me misfit on my brow, but I leave that matter to the Faculty.

"But the matter of the medal is distinctly personal and while I feel deeply honored by the wish of the Faculty, it is something I never expected. I never had an ambition, and at my age, especially in a position when I can *recogitabo annos meos in amaritudine animae meae,* I ought to think rather of the future *quinto è già il corso della vita mea.* I have led a sort of three-fold existence, known to many scholars in the country as one versed in American history, especially the French and Spanish period, Indian languages, ethnology and antiquities; to Catholics, as a writer historical and otherwise; and to a third set as an editor in New York whose name does not appear; and yet few are aware that the three are the same person. Others again know me as a bibliographer.

"I am trying to bear my confinement cheerfully, but I am afraid that my accident will make it impossible for me to be with you next month, as I fully intended to do unless you actually shut the door on me.

"It is my second disappointment of 1889. From the moment a pilgrimage to the Holy Land was proposed, I planned to go, but my two volumes have left me with such a host of obligations, that some months ago I reluctantly gave up all hope.

"If now I am to be denied this second Catholic pleasure I must make an act of resignation; but I shall feel that Georgetown University, the grand old Catholic column of learning, would welcome me and seek to honor me for my ordinary deserts.

"I trust the auspicious days will draw out much of the storied past that I could not reach, and enable me to make future editors of the *Life of Archbishop Carroll* treat more adequately the origin and early days of Georgetown."

The accident to which Dr. Shea refers happened on January 2, 1889, when on leaving a meeting of the United States Catholic Historical Society, he lost his footing while entering an elevator in the Trinity Building at 111 Broadway, New York City. Falling he injured his kneecap and ruptured one of the ligaments of his left leg. An ambulance was summoned and he was taken to the Chambers Street Hospital. The following day, he was brought to his home in Elizabeth, and telegrams soon began to arrive from his many friends, who feared that the accident would end his work on the *History*. He never fully recovered from the fall, and it was months before he could resume his post as editor of the Leslie publications. When he was ready to go back, he found that he had been superseded and forgotten. On February 4, 1889, he wrote Archbishop Corrigan, appending to his letter a list of the documents he wished to procure in the Propaganda Archives. His accident had increased his financial difficulties and he was greatly in debt at the time. A circular, which he issued brought him twenty more patrons, and with this lightening of his obligations, he wrote to the Archbishop:

"Accept my sincere thanks for your kind and encouraging letter, and my heartiest wishes and prayer for your prosperity. In the period which I am now studying (1815-1844) we have in this country very few documents for the first 15 or 20 years. There are no records of Bp. Connolly's or Bp. Egan's time, few of Bp. Conwell's, except those relating to the Hogan matter, absolutely nothing of Bp. Kelly's career as Bishop of Richmond. My only hope beyond chance facts picked up at random, is that some of the Rt. Rev. Bishops made reports on the state of their dioceses to the Prefect of the Propaganda. I annex a list which has a formidable look yet may bring only five or six reports. After the Catholic newspapers began and the *Annals* of the Propagation appeared, material became more accessible. Naturally I have been interested to give as full an account of Bishop Connolly's administration and life as I can. I have several letters and pamphlets but nothing official. If the $20 forwarded by Dr. McDonnell is not enough to cover the cost of making the copies I will remit whatever is needed. Burdened as you are with the care of a great diocese with so much to add to your cares and anxieties, I fell deeply reluctant to trespass on your kindness. Thanking you with all my heart for your constant protection and encouragement, I am with deep and sincere respect."

Archbishop Corrigan left soon afterwards for Rome, and while visiting the officials of the Sacred Congregation, then the head of all the American missions, he was enabled to arrange for the transcription of many of the documents Dr. Shea needed. All this took more money than Dr. Shea could afford. He had been given a set-back in 1886, when after all the business matters connected with his first volume were settled, he found that he had lost over fifteen hundred dollars by the publication of the book. His salary as editor was barely sufficient for the support of his little home, and now that the accident of January, 1889, had weakened his physical condition, he felt that he had fallen upon evil days. Sensitive to a high degree in all such matters, few outside his home knew the straits to which he was put to meet his current obligations, and on May 21, 1889, he wrote to Archbishop Corrigan the following note which tells plainly the position in which he was:

"Your Grace,

"In full consciousness of the many calls upon your time and thoughts I am most reluctant to make a personal appeal; but I am in a sore strait. When the matter of the *History of the Church* was proposed, it was suggested that I should withdraw from Leslie's establishment. This I was reluctant to do, as I regarded my position secure and permanent, but I leaned upon a straw. Leaving a meeting of the Committee of the Catholic Historical Society on the 2nd of January, I fell in stepping from an ill-constructed elevator and so injured my knee that I have been laid up and am now barely able to get about on crutches and even with them dare not attempt to walk in the street. During my enforced absence from the office, advantage was taken of this; although I continued to keep up my work. The prominence given to me directly and indirectly by my *History* prompted hostility, and I have recently been deprived of my position, a mere temporary position at a pittance being offered me.

"Nothing would be more congenial to me than Church work and if there be any position in the Chancery Office, Calvary Cemetery Office, or in connection with any of the institutions, where I could be sure of a moderate salary I should be only too grateful to Your Grace for enabling me to obtain it.

"I am able to work and willing. My aspirations are not high: and I do not ask to be a mere pensioner. If I can obtain a position in New York where I can earn my living, I can devote my leisure to the completion of the *History,* but if I am thrown upon precarious pieces of work, my labor on it must of necessity be fitful and uncertain. I commend the whole matter to Your Grace's kind consideration, and I feel certain from the friendly interest you have always manifested in me, that you will not feel offended at my thus intruding my private troubles on your attention. It was with great reluctance that I now address you, and do so only after efforts made in various directions, which have tended to discourage me.

"Whether you could exert influence in any other field than those I have named I do not know, but leaving the matter in Your Grace's hands, I remain with deep and sincere respect,

"Your Grace's obliged and grateful servant,

"JOHN GILMARY SHEA."

"Most Rev. M. A. Corrigan, D.D.,
Archbishop of New York."

The Centenary of Georgetown College took place in February of that year, and during the celebration, on February 22, 1889, the venerable *alma mater* of Catholic higher schools conferred on the distinguished historian the honorary degree of Doctor of Laws, and the medal. On one side was Dr. Shea's profile, with

THE GEORGETOWN MEDAL (1889)

his name running parallel with the edge, and on the reverse side, enclosed in half-wreaths of laurel and oak the following inscription:

GEORGETOWN
UNIVERSITY,
ON HER
HUNDREDTH ANNIVERSARY
TO THE
HISTORIAN
OF THE
CATHOLIC CHURCH
IN AMERICA
FOR HIS WORK
THE LIFE AND TIMES
OF
ARCHBISHOP CARROLL

Dr. Shea accepted the task of writing the *History of Georgetown College* which appeared in 1891.

Acting on the Archbishop's suggestion, Dr. Shea called to see Monsignor Donnelly in regard to his personal affairs. It is pathetic to be obliged to chronicle the fact that, even with the two volumes of the *History* to judge from, no one seems to have realized what Dr. Shea's age alone, he was then sixty-five, should have suggested; namely, a competence enabling him to finish the great work of his life without any of the anxieties connected with the burden of supporting his family. It is true, of course, that Dr. Shea's friends were dealing with a man who had all the legitimate pride a scholar of his distinction rightly possessed. It was not easy, perhaps to offer Dr. Shea a pension. He had never asked for charity, and like all men who give constantly without stint to others, he may have found it impossible to accept help when he needed it himself. At any rate, as the following letter (June 2, 1889) to the Archbishop shows, there was a ray of hope on the dark cloud that had gathered about the fireside in Elizabeth:

"I must thank you sincerely for your kind letter to Mgr. Donnelly in regard to my affairs. When I called on him yesterday my position was talked over at some length. It is far from my wish to be a pensioner or have a place made for me. I felt that if there were an opening anywhere for work which I was competent to do, Your Grace would exert influence in my favor . . . Another proposal has just been made to me. Mr. Ridder asks me to assume the editorship of the *Catholic News* and to give some days of the week to do it. As the editorship of a Catholic paper or periodical was never before offered me, I should not like to undertake it without Your Grace's sanction and entire approval. If I assumed the position it would be with the hope that I might, when occasion required, learn Your Grace's wishes as to the tone to be adopted, or the mode in which subjects should be treated. I can certainly conduct it prudently and temperately, how ably or successfully I cannot presume to say."

Dr. Shea assumed the editorship of the *News* in the summer of 1889, and in a statement to the subscribers laid down what he believed to be the function of the Catholic press in this country:

"To diffuse Catholic intelligence, to convey to every fireside, knowledge of what the Church is doing through her Head, and through the constituted government, what fellow-Catholics are doing to advance religion by societies, by united action, by rearing churches, schools, and institutions, by the use of the Press to diffuse truth and correct error, refute calumny and present real facts in order to disabuse those deluded by deep-seated prejudice, is simply giving each individual Catholic means at hand for an intelligent combat in the contest which the Church and her children are daily required to carry on; and fitting him to act his part nobly as a citizen of a free land. To carry at brief intervals to Catholic homes reading to interest and instruct, matter presented so attractive as to attract the young, especially from the flood of dangerous publications on every side, is also a great and important object of the Catholic press."

An effort was made in August, 1889, to call a meeting at Baltimore, in conjunction with the Catholic centennial, of the editors of all the Catholic papers in the country. In the printed circular sent out by L. W. Reilly, of Columbus, on September 21, 1889, the proposed formation of a Catholic Press Association was abandoned, owing to the fears expressed by Archbishops Elder and Ireland that questions might arise to disturb the harmony of the Congress. Dr. Shea declined to participate in the movement.

The movement which had been organized in the spring of 1889 to hold a great Catholic Congress in Baltimore on the occasion of the Centenary of the American Church, resulted in a notable gathering of Catholic lay leaders in November of that year. Former Governor John Lee Carroll, of Maryland, was chosen President, and the Committee on organization was composed of Messrs. William J. Onahan, Henry J. Spaunhorst, D. A. Rudd, John D. Keiley, and John Gilmary Shea. Henry Brownson, the chairman of the Committee on Papers, was the leading spirit in the centennial celebration, and Dr. Shea wrote to him in May, 1889, thanking him for the honor conferred on him. "Unfortunately," he says, "it will be impossible for me to meet the other gentlemen of the Committee on the day named, as I am still unable to walk, having fallen and sustained a severe injury in January. In subsequent meetings I hope to be able to take an active part."

Mr. Brownson had suggested that he prepare for the celebration a paper on the part Catholic laymen had played in the growth of the United States. On June 25, 1889, Dr. Shea replied:

"I would like to gratify the Committee and mankind generally by such a paper as is proposed, but, your father apart, what have we Catholics done in the domain of literature, science, or art, that can be paraded? None of the great poets, orators, historians, leaders in natural or medical sciences, in painting, sculpture, architecture, in great inventions, belonged to us. Will it not do more harm than good to get up and parade fifth-rate people and extol them as paragons of excellence? If I could only see my way clear, I should be happy to go at the paper, but it is in my mind like the chapter on 'Snakes in Ireland,' or Tagliaferro's Chapter on what the Constitution says against the right of a State to secede. I really think seriously that some other topic ought to be selected. There are subjects it seems to me more safe."

Mr. Brownson then asked him to prepare a paper on Catholic Congresses, which eventualy Dr. Shea did, and this was the opening paper read at the celebration on November 11, 1889. It was the first time in the history of the nation that representative lay Catholic met to discuss the general interests of the Church, mainly the relation to the Holy See and to the government of the United States. Dr. Shea called attention to the repeated violation of constitutional rights by the government in the matter of Catholic property, to the serious condition of the Catholic Indians, which needed "prompt" and "energetic action," to the invasion of the rights of the Catholic parents in the question of religious education, and to the necessity of counteracting error, especially by means of the Catholic press.

Dr. Shea lost confidence in the value of the Congress after he heard "the tame and meaningless words" of the resolution passed regarding the independence of the Holy See. He turned to Bishop Maes, of Covington, who sat beside him, "to express my astonishment and grief," he writes to Father Audran, of Vincennes, on May 21, 1890. "I am glad personally," he continues, "that I am on record as speaking clearly. I translated and printed in the *Catholic News* a very remarkable pamphlet on the question which I got from Rome. It swarmed with decisive arguments. I believe in speaking out and speaking out boldly. Alas! we see now what we lost in Mr. McMaster. In the Catholic press in the United States I do not see an editor with American pluck and Roman back-bone. Now, late in life, I am connected with a Catholic paper, but a man of sixty-six is rather too old to learn new ways. Thirty years ago I might have done good service but the timid feared me. I am now working mainly on my *History of the Church."*

At the close of the Catholic Congress of Baltimore in 1889, the prelates and members of this historic assembly journeyed to Washington to assist in laying the cornerstone of the first building of the Catholic University of America. Dr. Shea did not take part in this ceremony. None among the prominent laymen present had given proof of a more profound interest in the new institution of higher learning. In several of Shea's articles on the proposed American Catholic university, there will be found what is undoubtedly the clearest of all the numerous plans suggested for its origin and administration. Dr. Shea had been consulted by Bishop Keane on the new foundation and there was little doubt in his mind that he would be asked to take a place in the original faculty. As the first of its teachers in American history, the Catholic University would have immediately gained a prestige which the passing years would have augmented and enhanced.

The offer did not come, however, and Dr. Shea felt very keenly the silence which settled down upon his own suggestions for the new home of higher scholarship.

What his own scholarly tastes might have contributed to the University in these earliest years is seen in one of his articles in the *American Catholic Quarterly Review* for July, 1885. "This country," he wrote, "is practically without a great University. Spanish America boasted of some in other days, but they are gone, or exist only as a shadow of former greatness . . . the collegiate institutions in the English colonies, out of which our Republic has grown, were all based on the plan of the Universities at Oxford and Cambridge, as those seats of learning came forth dwarfed and crippled from the destroying and study-despising epoch of the Reformation. As the Universities lost with Catholicity the very idea of their creation, the copies were indeed far removed from the true ideal. The narrowness and insular character of the training and knowledge imparted by the universities in the seventeenth and eighteenth centuries was strikingly seen in the vast difference between the cultured Catholic gentlemen who had been trained in a continental university, and the Protestant squire whose education was limited to Oxford and Cambridge."

This bold statement left no doubts in the minds of his readers what Dr. Shea expected from the Catholic University of America. His ideal was a great central school to which well-equipped graduates of our Catholic seminaries and colleges would come for advanced study in theology, philosophy, jurisprudence, letters, arts, and sciences. He, too, feared the opposition to the great project which was then apparent in ecclesiastical circles, but "if it is not cramped and thwarted by half-hearted assent and real opposition," then he saw in vision coming from its halls "a host of intellectually trained priests and laymen, whose influence will be felt in every department of thought, who can make the American contributions to literature, science and the arts instinct with the life and the light that can come from but one source, Divine Truth."

Meanwhile, the third volume was not neglected. On September 9, 1889, Dr. Shea wrote to Archbishop Corrigan: "Learning from Dr. McDonnell that you have again written to Rome to obtain the reports that are so vitally necessary to my work, I hasten to express my sincere thanks. I have been gathering material and laboriously wading through papers to make notes, but in the terribly straightened position into which I have been thrown, the progress in actually writing my third volume has been slow. The appearance of two rival histories, which, of course, draw greatly from my researches, but which are pushed actively through canvassers, will make the completion of my *History* very difficult financially, as I anticipated no such ungenerous competition when I undertook the work."

After his return from the centennial celebration, Dr. Shea fell ill, and it was February, 1890, before he could resume work on the third volume of the *History*. Father Patrick Corrigan, who had stood by him in all his difficulties, now realized that unless Dr. Shea's immediate distress were removed, the work could never be finished. With the help of some friends, he finally collected the sum of one thousand dollars and sent it as a preliminary subsidy to Dr. Shea, who immediately informed the proprietor of the *Catholic News* that he wished to end his editorial duties, in order to devote himself entirely to the volumes which remained to be written. Father Corrigan's generous co-operation relieved Shea of all anxiety, and for the first time in his long life of sixty-six years, his mind was free from financial worry.

There was an interesting historical announcement in the *Catholic News* for May 4, 1890, which tells us in retrospect the story of the *History* up to that time:

"Some years since I was invited to write the History of the Catholic Church in this country, and subscriptions were advanced by several of the hierarchy, clergy and laity sufficient to cover the cost of the volumes as they were undertaken. Of these generous friends nearly one-third have already passed from this world. Two volumes were written and published. Soon after the appearance of the second volume, 'The Life and Times of Archbishop Carroll,' an accident laid me up for months a cripple. Though I endeavored successfully in this state to fulfil my usual editorial duties, I was deprived of nearly my whole income by an unjust and cruel act that I never anticipated. While in this position the proprietor of the *Catholic News* offered me the editorial charge of his paper, and, aided by the intelligent and well-informed staff connected with that journal, I have till the present time labored to meet his expectations and those of the Catholic body.

"Meanwhile my History was virtually suspended, beyond the collection of material and studies of particular phases of periods. Understanding this, some friends in the clergy of the State where I reside made an effort to enable me to lay aside all other work and apply myself to the completion of the History. Since the first of January I have done nothing else, except the editorial work of the *Catholic News,* notwithstanding which, my third volume is so far advanced that it will appear early this summer unless some unforeseen event intervenes.

"I notified the proprietor of the *Catholic News* of the position of affairs, and of my relinquishment of all other work. As he had made heavy outlay, based on my continuance as editor of the *News,* he had felt great reluctance to sever the connection which will involve loss, and require a change in the management of the paper.

"For my own part I should without hesitation retire at once from the editorial chair, did I find that it interfered with my special work. Hitherto it has been no obstacle, but, on the contrary, by the wide circulation it enjoys, the *News* brings me in contact with Catholics in all parts of the country, enables me to see all the Catholic journals, and profit by all historical reminiscences, biographical sketches and the like. It has also enabled me to obtain important and valuable material. My presence in the office is limited to two days, and the change of scene for that short time is beneficial to my health.

"My great desire is to complete the History of the Church. To it I will sacrifice all other matters, and even the editorship of the *News,* if it proves the slightest bar, shall be relinquished on due notice, whenever I feel and my kind friends see that it retards the work."

This announcement, he felt, would leave him free to resign his post on the *Catholic News* the moment he felt he could not carry on the work without interfering with the *History.*

On May 5, 1890, Dr. Shea wrote to Father Corrigan:

"I inserted in the last number of the *News* a statement which you have seen, as Mr. Ridder promised to send you copies. It defines my position and leaves me free to withdraw whenever I find it necessary. Last week I did an immense deal of work at Baltimore, and today I hear of a large batch of documents coming from Rome. My volume, so far as my actual material goes, is half done, and I am arranging to begin the printing at once. I got out volumes I and II by night work, about 25 hours a week, after a hard day's work in the office in New York. Now by the help coming from you and the large-hearted friends who have responded to you, I have devoted 55 hours a week to the History, and I certainly can complete the three volumes in two years or very little more. The connection with the *News* is a diversion that helps rather than retards the work, and of course when my book is completed, leaves me a foothold for the future. My chief aim is now to close up the work on the history with as little delay as possible, so as not to tax the generosity of my friends a day longer than is necessary. If, however, my name on Ridder's paper at all affects your appeal, it must come off and my work there cease."

Before September had passed, Father Corrigan had sent to Dr. Shea a third subsidy of one thousand dollars. In acknowledging the receipt of the same, Dr. Shea wrote (September 26, 1890) :

"While enclosing receipt for $1,000, being the third payment made by you this year, I must express more deeply than ever how much I owe you personally and all Catholics owe to your disinterested exertions and to the generous friends whom you have interested in the Church History of this country.

"The accident which befell me and the consequence it entailed, made it very difficult for me to continue the work, and I began to feel that no one for a century would attempt to go so systematically over the whole ground. Your action enabled me to complete the work as I projected it. Besides adding steadily to my stock of documents from Rome and collections in dioceses here, I have acquired many necessary books, newspapers, pamphlets, letters of Bishops, priests, religious, giving me a rich mine of material. Since the commencement of the year I have labored steadily on my third volume, and have nearly six hundred pages in type, so that I can certainly issue next month. I shall then set out for the West in search of documents and letters, and on my return, begin writing the fourth volume, which I hope, God willing, to complete by the first of May.

"The fifth and concluding volume I aim and trust to have entirely written by the end of the year, so as to issue it early in 1892. My aim is to be able to show the whole work brought to a conclusion before the Columbus centenary. In the volume about to appear I shall express my gratitude for the appreciation already manifested in my work, but I hope to receive from you a complete list of those who so nobly co-operate with you that I may dedicate my fifth volume and the work it crowns to those who deserve to be remembered as long as the work can preserve their memory."

When autumn came, Dr. Shea felt strong enough to make the journey to Notre Dame University for the purpose of completing his researches among the valuable collection which Professor Edwards had gathered there. On his return to Elizabeth, he wrote to Father Sorin (November 24, 1890): "Returning to my home, after you, with such kindness, escorted me to the train, I feel it a duty to thank you with all the sincerity of my heart for your condescension and favor during my stay at Notre Dame. Much as I had heard of your institution, and with some conceptions formed, I was prepared for what I actually beheld. The work of your life inspired by a love of God and our Lady guided by such a clear insight into what the condition of Catholics in this country required, has produced indeed, institutions which in their thoroughness of literary, scientific and practical courses are unequalled; and you have the secret of imbuing all around you with a sense of religion, refinement and art, that is not easy to describe, but which is felt at every step. The incalculable good that your University has effected and will for years continue to produce has never been fully appreciated. In my soul came the deep feeling of regret that in my early days Providence had not guided me to you, to labor under your direction these years of a comparatively wasted life. What a glory it would be to me to have taken part in so much good accomplished for the salvation of souls, and the elevation of our people. With the deepest veneration and gratitude for the kindness and fatherly interest so recently evinced, crowning many former acts, I shall ever be your devoted, thankful Son and Servant in Xt."

On All Saints', 1890, the third volume was through the press, although it was not on sale until February of the next year, owing to delay in the bindery. It carried the narrative from the death of Archbishop Carroll to the Fifth Provincial Council of Baltimore in 1843. In the preface to the volume, Dr. Shea relates the story of the intrigue which was successfully planned by those in the Frank Leslie concern who were opposed to the Catholic Faith and which deprived him of his only means of support. He then thanks Father P. Treacy of Burlington, N. J., for the financial support he had secured in 1889 after the accident—Cardinal Gibbons headed the list with a gift of fifty dollars "in favor of so worthy a gentleman, who has spent himself in the cause of religion and historical truth,"—and then offers the volume to Father Treacy in dedication and gratitude. To Father Patrick Corrigan he announced in the same preface that when the *History* was completed, the whole work would be dedicated to him and to his generous co-operators. "I trust," he writes, "that the Catholic public will accept this *History of the Church* with some of the kindness which has prompted such a self-sacrificing spirit to enable me to complete it." The inside cover of the third volume contained a facsimile engraving of the Georgetown medal of the previous year.

The third volume is divided into six Books. The first Book treats of the Province of Baltimore from 1815 to 1829. Book two deals with the Dioceses of Louisiana and the Floridas, New Orleans, and St. Louis and the Vicariate of Alabama. Book three consists of two chapters on the First Provincial Council of Baltimore, and on the Growth of Anti-Catholic Feeling. Book four returns to the Province of Baltimore and gives the history of that diocese and of its suffragan Sees from 1829 to 1843. The fifth Book returns to the Middle West and Louisiana, and the last Book treats of Texas. The arrangement is unsatisfactory, and it makes an impression on the reader of notes hastily put together in geographical classification and then strung together into a connected whole. The whole of the United States at the time still comprised one ecclesiastical Province, that of Baltimore, and the volume would have gained in strength and clarity had Dr. Shea kept to a less rigid outline. But there is nothing of importance missing. Every detail of Catholic life in these stirring years is told, either in the text or in footnotes, and the volume is, like all Dr. Shea's work, a mine for the research student.

During these seven years of intense activity on his *History,* Dr. Shea was able to issue several volumes of importance to the Church of the United States. His translation of Father Martin's *Life of Father Jogues,* which had appeared in Paris in 1875, was published in 1885, and quickly became a popular book among Catholics in this country. The basis of Shea's translation was an incomplete one made by Father Finotti, which Dr. Shea found so faulty that he did the whole work over. Shea's volume was published as a thank-offering to Blessed Isaac Jogues, and all the profits accruing from the sale of the book went to the Chapel of Our Lady of Martyrs at Auriesville, New York.

Another work, which is entirely unworthy of Dr. Shea's great skill, is his *Hierarchy of the Catholic Church in the United States,* published in 1886 (pp. 445). Richard H. Clarke's *Lives of the Deceased Bishops of the Catholic Church in the United States* appeared in two volumes (New York, 1872), but the want was felt of a handy volume containing short biographies of all the bishops for popular reading. Only the strongest necessity of meeting his obligations induced Dr. Shea to prepare his *Hierarchy* as well as other popular volumes such as the *Pictorial Lives of the Saints,* (pp. 138, New York, 1888), and *The Defenders of our Faith,* (pp. 678, New York, 1892). He was one of those writers whose scholarship was too perfect for popular works of this kind.

One short essay which belongs to this period and which he meant to be the basis of an important work is his *Bibliography of the Councils, Synods and Statutes of the Catholic Church in the United States.* (1890). For years he had collected the printed Acts and Decrees of all the American Councils and Synods, and his correspondence shows that he intended to complete his collection and then to publish a series of volumes containing all these important enactments with historical notes to elucidate the text. In January, 1887, he appealed to Cardinal Gibbons to foster this series of volumes. "God has given Your Eminence," he says, "the great gift of reaching the hearts of the people, and I feel that it will increase the great merit already acquired as one of those *qui erudiunt omnes."* The idea of a printed collection of these volumes appealed to many of our bishops, and Dr. Shea

was constantly urged to begin the work by publishing all the
official acts of Archbishop Carroll.

Dr. Shea had intended to make a second visit to Notre Dame
University in the spring of 1891, in order to complete his notes
for his fourth volume. For this part of his *History* (1844-1866),
he was obliged to depend to a larger extent than he wished upon
the Catholic newspapers published in various parts of the country. By January, 1891, he had read and indexed eighty volumes
of these old newspapers, magazines, annals, and reports, and still
had about eighty more to do, together with all the local and
State histories.

To Monsignor (Cardinal) Farley, he wrote on May 2, 1891:
"We have had a sick time here recently, and Mrs. Shea has
been very dangerously ill. Today we can see encouraging im-
provement, although we are by no means free from anxiety."
He tells Bishop Gilmour of Cleveland on February 9, 1891, how
all this anxiety had hindered him but that he had then settled
down to write the volume which was to be his last. Monsignor
Farley wrote encouraging letters from time to time, and Dr. Shea
needed such support, for he knew, as he says, that he was on
"delicate ground," since his fourth volume would deal with some
personages in the Church still living. In another interesting
letter ('April 27, 1891), to his great friend, James C. Pilling, the
ethnologist and bibliographer of the Indian tribes, who had been
stricken that year with a fatal disease which was to carry him
off in his prime (1846-1895), Dr. Shea says: "Your information
gave me a shock, limping myself and doomed to limp, for my
muscles do not gain strength.   I can scarcely bring myself to
believe that one who like yourself seemed a picture of health
should be steadily losing the power of locomotion. We are both
in the hands of God." To Father George Houck, he wrote (May
12, 1891): "I am weak. My stomach is not inclined to work.
My lameness continues. My eyesight is gone in one eye, and I
get low-spirited at times. So you see I have received more than
the old woman's warnings which Death promised her before he
came in person. It cannot be long before I drop the 'and' out of
the Hail Mary and say: 'Pray for us sinners now at the hour of
our death.'"

Among the problems facing him at this time was the disposal of his library. One of his friends, Father John J. Dougherty, interested himself in the matter, and at his suggestion Dr. Shea printed this announcement containing a catalogue of his books, pamphlets and manuscripts:

MY DEAR FATHER DOUGHERTY :

IN answer to your note requesting some memoranda about my Library I will state as follows:

The Library has been collected almost exclusively to bring together books relating to the History of the Catholic Church in the United States, and those countries directly connected with it.

Beginning with the discovery of Vinland by the Northmen it has Torfaeus' Vinland, in Latin, with the recent English translation, works by DaCosta, Horsford, and others on the Northmen.

The discovery by Columbus is represented by the Regiomontanus Almanac, 1489; Ruchamer, 1508; the Letters of Peter Martyr, the Giustiniani Psalter, containing the first life of Columbus, 1572; Barlow's fac-simile of First Voyage, privately printed; Scyllacius, Third Voyage, privately printed by James Lenox; Harrisse's Notes and Work on the Genoa Bank, both privately printed; Lives by Ferdinand Columbus, Roselly de Lorgues, Tarducci; the discussion as to the Coffin discovered at Santo Domingo in a series of pamphlets.

The early voyages and discoveries on our coast by Catholics are shown in Ramusio, 1565; Montanus, Grynaeus, Thevet's Cosmographie, 1585; and France Antarctique, Porcacchi and Ortelius, Gemma Phrysius, DeLaet; the discussion as to Verazzani by Murphy, Brevoort, Da-Costa; Harrisse's Cabot, etc.

The Spanish Mission-work at the South, in Florida, New Mexico, Texas, Arizona and California is described in Mendoza's China, 1585, etc.; Montoya's New Mexico, 1602; Benavides, 1630; Perea, Vetancurt, Torquemada, Davila, Barcia, Menendes, Historia del Colegio Apostolico; all the Lives of Ven. Father Margil, Process of his Canonization; Life of Father Juniper Serra, Maria de Agreda, Mistica Cuidad dal de Dios and Correspondence; Alegre's History of the Society of Jesus, Tanner's Societas Militans; Palou's work, the Tres Cartes on the Dominican Missions, Hernanez, Coleccion de Bulas, Escudero's Sonora and Chihuahua; Pino's New Mexico, Azipe's Texas, De Onis' Memorial; Coleccion Ecclesiastica Mejicana, several works of Ayeta: the Sermon on the Martyrs of the Colorado. Many of these works are of extreme rarity. There are also Alaman's History of Mexico, Veytia, works on Central America, Porto Rico, etc.

On Canada connecting with the early missions in Maine, New York, Michigan, Ohio, Indiana, and Illinois, Wisconsin, etc., there are Cartier's Voyages, (Tross' reprints), Champlain's Voyages, Paris and Quebec reprints; L'Escarbot, Tross reprint; the Jesuit Relations 14 out of 36 originals, and the Quebec reprint; Ragueneau's Life of La Mère Cathérine, original; Traités avec les Sauvages, original; several eclects, original; Creuxius, Historia Canadensis, original; Le Clercq's Gaspesie; Etablissement de la Foi, imperfect; Hennepin's Various Voyages, Le Houtan, Le Beau, Bossu, etc., Marquette's Voyages, Rich's and Lenox's with a curious Dutch edition; Joutel's Voyage in French and Spanish; Juchereau, Histoire de l'hotel Dieu, Charlevoix, Vie de la Mère Marie de l'Incarnation, and other lives; Quebec Rituel; Histories of Canada by Charlevoix, De la Potherie, Ferland, Maillon, Garneau; Sagard's Grand Voyage, original and reprint; Sagard's Historie du Canada; Lives of Ven. Bishop Laval by La Tour and others; Life of Bp. St. Valier; Historical works of Abbé Casgrain, Memoires des Commissionaires; works on Nova Scotia; Pastoral Letters of Bishops and Archbishops of Quebec. Early Jesuit Relations printed or reprinted privately by Mr. James Lenox and Dr. O'Callaghan; the Cramoisy Series. Works on Louisiana by Le Page du Pratz, Dumont, La Harpe, Laval, the famous memorial original, Champigny, Margry's Collections; Quebec Documents; Byrmner's Archive Reports.

For Maryland missions and the development of the Church, Dodd's History of the Church in England, Flanagan's, Olivers Collections, and Biography, the Records of the Society of Jesus by Brother Foley; Brennan's History of the Church in Ireland; Cogan's History of the Diocese of Meath; Life of Right Rev. Dr. Doyle; Laws of Maryland; White's Journal, Relations of Maryland.

Works on the French co-operation in the Revolution are largely represented.

Lives of Archbishop Carroll and *all* other biographies of Catholic Bishops or Priests, or religious in this country published in any language, making more than 150 volumes.

Histories of dioceses, churches, colleges, parishes, that have appeared in this country in English, German, or French. Many works on Religious orders, their rules, ceremonials, etc. Of the Catholic Councils, Synods, Statutes issued in the various dioceses, there are about 100, a collection that cannot be equalled.

A set of the Annales de la Propagation de la Foi, a set of the Quebec Annales, a set of the Berichte der Leopolden Stiftung, with many works on the Indian missions by Father DeSmet and others.

Of the early printed Catholic books in this country, I have 205, the greater part of those described in Finotti's Bibliographia Catholica Americana, and 38 that were unknown to him, including some of the earliest and rarest. The library contains all the Catholic Bibles, Testaments, etc., printed in this country described in Shea's Bibliography of Catholic Bibles. The Catholic Newspapers, Magazines and Reviews printed in the United States amount now to 489 volumes, a collection that seems incredible to some who know the difficulty of obtaining them.

The Collection of Catholic pamphlets is very large, probably 3000 in all, and embraces many of a general character, on the School Question,

Freedom of Worship, Lectures, Discussions, with Pastoral Letters and others relating to single dioceses in the United States.

For collateral study there are Histories of the United States by Bancroft, McMaster, Spencer, the rare publications of the Bradford Club and Prince Society; the best history of each one of the States, some extremely rare, Horsmanden's Negro Plot; publications of the New York, Wisconsin, Pennsylvania, New Hampshire and other Historical Societies; a share in the Publication Fund of the New York Historical Society and the volumes issued by it; the Historical Magazine, Magazine of Pennsylvania Historical Society, New England Historical Genealogical Register, etc.

There are also books of Travel touching on Catholic matters, Controversies, local histories bearing on Catholic churches, institutions, etc.

The set of Catholic Almanacs is complete, including Field's, 1817; Power's, 1822; and the rival editions where two appeared, and the local ones issued during Civil War.

There are rare early works not connected with this country, but in place in a Catholic Library, Bible of 1494, Testament of 1506; Mamotrectus or Explanation of Hard Words in the Bible, 1483; a work on the Mass about 1470, with the old form of the Hail Mary written on last page, and defaced by some Reformer; De Triplice Vita, 1489; Works showing popular religious teaching before the Reformation—De Burgo's Pupilla Oculi, De Eruditione Christe Fidelium, Manipulus Curatorum, etc., the original edition of Blessed Thomas More's Utopia; several early printed Catholic works from Continental presses; Pentateuch in Hebrew, Spanish, with prayers, Jewish prayer books, and the two earliest books issued in the Irish character at Rome.

Besides the Bible of 1494, there is the edition of the Bible issued in 1592 by Pope Clement VIII. which was made the standard. This is now extremely rare, and took me years to find; the edition of 1593, and that issued under Pius IX. from the Propaganda Press; the Bible de Vence, Latin and French; Allioli's Bible, Latin and German; the original Douay and Rheims Bible, 1582, 1609; the second edition by Consturier, Rouen; Witham's New Testament, 2 vols., with one volume or an edition unknown to Cotton; Nary's New Testament, excessively rare; Blessed John Moher's Penitential Psalms; first edition of the Greek Testament in United States, etc.

The collection of books relating to the Indian tribes with works in Indian languages is very large. Many of these bear on Catholic missions. It embraces a full set, and, perhaps, the only full set of the reports of the Indian Department, and many reports, travels, expeditions, tribal histories and mission accounts now rare. The works in and on Indian languages number 380, and form one of the largest collections of the kind in the United States. This part, if not considered desirable, could be easily disposed of for $1000.

Bibliography is represented by Sabin's American Bibliography, about half the numbers; Bibliographies of the Indian languages by Pilling,

Cotton's English Bibles and Rheims and Douay, O'Callaghan's American Bibles, Catalogues of the New York State Library, Wisconsin Historical Society, etc., Corwin's, Squier's, O'Callaghan's, Finotti's, Brinley's, Barlow's, Brayton Ives', and many other large libraries; Bibliographical works on the Jesuits, Franciscans, etc.

There are, besides, general histories of the Church and of the Missions, with many works on Protestant sects useful for reference.

Besides many books of miscellaneous character, the library comprises an entensive collection of documents relating to the History of the Catholic Church in America, originals or copies made in Rome, France, Spain, England, copies of early parish registers, letters, etc. There is also a large collection of autograph letters, embracing papers and documents signed and issued by many of the Popes, letters of Cardinals, famous men, monarchs, most of the Presidents of the United States, Vice Presidents, Cabinet officers and others, with most of the Catholic Bishops of the United States from the Most Rev. John Carroll to the present time.

Many curious relics of early Catholic times will also be found there.

I think this synopsis will give you what you desire, an idea of my Library, and I remain, dear Rev. Father, with great respect,

Your Sincere Friend,

JOHN GILMARY SHEA.

There is a letter to Father Dougherty, dated May 10, 1891, which gives us Dr. Shea's views and incidentally the information that two Catholic institutions had approached him on the matter:

"I am greatly indebted to you for your interest in myself personally which I appreciate fully. I shrink however from any farther appeal such as Father Corrigan and Father Treacy have made. Rev. Mr. McGean spoke to me in consequence of a letter of His Grace Archbishop Corrigan to him. I then said that all I asked was some patrons to replace the fifteen who have died. It would be better to aid in circulating the book. Two Catholic Institutions have made proposals to secure my library. It is the largest and fullest collection of books, pamphlets, periodicals, newspapers, documents, autographs, portraits and views relating to the history of the Catholic Church in this Country that will ever be got together. My books, pamphlets, bound newspapers, and magazines amount in all to about 13,000, so far as I can judge, and could not be obtained in twenty years' search. It is worth $10,000. I should like to see it in some Catholic Institution where it would be preserved and increased, but I am his great work for American Catholic history that he meant to finish the *History,* if it took his last ounce of strength. In reality, it did, for with the coming of the New Year, 1892, he worked with the consciousness that every hour counted, and that it was to be a race till the end.

CHAPTER VIII

THE END

February 22, 1892)

John Gilmary Shea had now reached his sixty-eighth year. He realized, better than all around him, that he had never fully recovered from the accident of 1889. Two purposes dominated the heroic struggle he was to make from New Year's Day to Washington's Birthday, in 1892. The first of these was the completion of his *History of the Catholic Church in the United States.* As originally announced in 1885, there were to be five volumes to the work, the fifth volume bearing the title *The Church on the Pacific Coast.* As the work progressed, he found it more logical to combine the third, fourth and fifth volumes into two, the first to contain the narrative of our Catholic history from 1815 to 1844; the second, from 1844 to 1866. He had no intention of carrying the narrative farther than the Second Plenary Council of Baltimore (1866). The remainder, from the Second to the Third Plenary Councils (1866-1884), and from 1884 to his own day, he believed should be left to his successors in the field to accomplish. He felt that this period (1866-1892), which saw some of the most intricate problems the Catholic Church in America has yet had to solve, should be allowed to undergo "the mellowing influence of time," in order that the events which literally crowd its years "might be judged in a calmer mood and in juster proportion."

In one way, it is to be regretted that his life was not prolonged for another decade at least; for, had he been able to narrate our history, as no one but Shea could narrate it then, we should have a completely rounded-out chronicle of the four hundred years of American history which came to an end on October 12, 1892. Another regret may well be added to this. In 1892, the literature of the American history was almost in the same unsatisfactory state, as when John Lingard began (1819), the publication of his *History of England.* The revised edition (1880-1882) of Hildreth's *History of the United States* was for all its six volumes too meagre and too partisan to last. John

Elizabeth NJ 18 Feb /82

Dear

I have assigned the property insured by the Manchester Fire Assurance Co on the Mansion [house] Rahway to Sophie S Shea. Please have policy made to correspond.

Yours truly

John G. Shea

Woodward [Sherwood] &Co

SHEA'S LAST LETTER

Marshall had failed in his *Life of Washington* to give us an accurate estimate of the spirit of colonial liberty and had blundered in his interpretation of the political forces centering about the repeal of the Stamp Act. George Bancroft's *History of the United States*, the tenth volume of which brought the narrative down to 1789, had in spite of its fascinating style lost sight of the deeper effects of our colonial life upon the growth of our national institutions.

There was need of a history of the United States, written with that unbiased accuracy which John Lingard possessed above all his contemporaries in England. It is not too forcible a word to say that John Gilmary Shea alone might have given us a history of the United States that would have analyzed with perfection every factor, social, religious and political, that had gone into the building of the American nation. We need not go all the way with one who was then the foremost Catholic layman in the United States, in saying that "it is simply impossible for the most liberal Protestant writer to treat with entire fairness any Catholic subject," but we can hold in all security of judgment that the scholar who had revealed to Americans generally and to Catholics in particular the share in the formation of the nation taken by those of the Catholic Faith, was prepared as were few other historians of his day to translate the entire past into a record which like Lingard's would bear the brunt of criticism and approach the ideal standard work upon the subject.

All through the three thousand pages of his *History*, Dr. Shea not only proved his right to be considered one of America's foremost historians, but there is a haunting quality in his volumes which hints that once he had completed his great work of depicting on the canvas of the past the story of Catholicism in the United States, the larger field would have found in him one of the most mature students of the time. Had he but lived to do this greater work, his place in American historiography would be that of a master; his voluminous writings would have placed beyond cavil the claims those of the Catholic Faith rightly make for a preponderant share in the nation's rise and growth; his own scholarship would have reached its full flowering; and we should be witnesses in our own day of a fairer and juster estimate of the moral, intellectual, and political gifts Catholicism has made to the nation.

That task remains to be done. Dr. Shea has not only shown the way in his *Catholic Missions,* in his translation of De Courcy's *Essais,* and in his own *History,* but has given us in the hundred and more works which he published from 1852 to 1892, a treasure house of facts and suggestions, guides to source-material, and the invaluable judgments his long years of study fashioned on almost every phase of our national and religious history.

Knowing that he was leaving this greater task undone, Dr. Shea's mind was preoccupied with a second problem during these last months of his life; namely, the preservation of his collection of manuscripts, pamphlets, and books for the future Catholic historians of the land.

There were several places in the United States at that time where such a precious collection could have been safely housed. The Catholic University of America was unprepared in 1892 to be the home of a special library of this nature. The study of Church history was just beginning at the University under the late Bishop Thomas O'Gorman, D.D., and the present Rector, Bishop Thomas J. Shahan, D.D. The American Catholic Historical Society of Philadelphia had then completed eight years of active service to the cause of American history. Its present spacious home was not purchased until 1895, but as we have seen the officers and managers of the Society endeavored to secure Dr. Shea's collection as a nucleus for its own "library and cabinet," as it was called in those days.

The University of Notre Dame had established through Professor James Farnham Edwards a central Catholic Archives of America. Many of the bishops had entered into Edwards' plans, and he made a journey through the Middle West and the East gathering up all monumental and archival sources for our Catholic history.

Dr. Shea profited, as we have seen, by the Catholic Archives of America and visited the University of Notre Dame in order to study this material. On another occasion he wrote to Mr. Edwards: "Your wonderfully kind loan has arrived safely and is a deluge of historical material, a perfect mine of facts, estimates and judgments. Many of these letters have been in several hands, and how little they have made of them! There are some where every line is a volume to one who understands. De Courcy had some of them, Bishop Bayley had them for years, Archbishop Hughes also had them. I recognize by Bishop Bayley's endorsement some of the Bruté papers so long in his hands and part of which perished by fire. You possess in what you have gathered more material for a real history of the Church in this country during the present century than was ever dreamt of. Your own zeal and labor as a collector, guided by intelligent love of Church and country, has been rewarded by great results. Yet I hope that it is only a beginning. I recognize more thoroughly now what you have done and, properly supported, may still do. You have created a new line, and your zeal has saved much from decay and destruction."

But the problem which faced Dr. Shea was not only to find a safe place for his collection but also to make its transfer from his own possession a medium of financial assistance to his wife and children. Eventually, at a considerable outlay, the Society of Jesus secured the valuable John Gilmary Shea collection of books and manuscripts.

Dr. Shea lay dying on February 19, 1892, when Father J. Havens Richards, S.J., then President of Georgetown University, came to Elizabeth, to secure Dr. Shea's signature to the agreement between himself and the Society for the transfer of the collection to the University. On his way back to Georgetown, Father Richards wrote from Baltimore (February 21) begging Mrs. Shea and her daughters to be courageous before the trial which was then recognized to be inevitable. "Let me impress upon you," he wrote to Isabel Shea, "the absolute necessity for yourself, your mother and your sister, to take proper rest, and not allow yourselves to be agitated and distressed. If our dear Lord intends to take your father, that is no reason why all the rest of the family should kill themselves with nervous worry and distress. Dr. Shea himself is very calm, submissive, and sensible; and if he can be so at this great moment, you ought all to be able to bring yourselves to the same frame of mind. This is important even for his sake, and I hope you will endeavor to carry it out. If I had any authority, I would order you all to try to be resigned and tranquil, and to take a little sleep, or at least, try to, by turns, if necessary, every afternoon."

Dr. Shea had shown the first signs of his approaching end on February 13, when a chill that lasted more than an hour made him put aside the proof sheets of his last volume and go to bed. He recovered, however, and the next morning, Sunday, though unable to attend Mass, he was with the family at breakfast. The following day he was able to rise, and Father Eugene Carroll, of St. Mary's Church, who was called in, urged Mrs. Shea to tell her husband of his serious condition. This was done immediately, and Dr. Shea asked for the Last Sacraments, which he received the next day, February 16. After Father Carroll had left, Dr. Shea forced himself back to the desk in his study and worked at the proofs until he had finished them. On Wednesday Father Corrigan, the loyal friend of his late years, came, and on Thursday Monsignor Farley came over from New York, to bid him good-bye. On Friday, Bishop Wigger of Newark came to give Dr. Shea the last blessing, and on Monday, February 21, he was very much elated by the reception of a cablegram from Rome with the blessing of Pope Leo XIII, which Archbishop Corrigan had requested.

When it was seen on Sunday afternoon that Dr. Shea could not last much longer, the family knelt around his bedside, saying the prayers for the dying. Dr. Shea answered these prayers to the very end. He died at seven minutes to four in the morning of February 22, his last act being an attempt to put the rosary beads, given to him years before by Cardinal Gibbons, to his lips. Around his bedside when he died, were Mrs. Shea, his daughters, Ida and Emma Isabel, Jessie Tenny, the daughter of Judge Tenny, whose second wife was Sarah Brownson, daughter of Dr. O. A. Brownson, and Charles Ives, the grand-nephew of Dr. Levi Silliman Ives, former Episcopal Bishop of North Carolina, whose conversion to the Faith had caused so much surprise in 1852.

Dr. Shea's funeral took place on Friday, February 26, from St. Mary's Church, Elizabeth, New Jersey. Solemn pontifical Mass was celebrated by Bishop Wigger, of Newark, assisted by Father J. Havens Richards, S.J., President of Georgetown University, Rev. Patrick Corrigan, Rev. Eugene Carroll, Father

John H. Finnegan, S.J., Vice President of St. Peter's College, Jersey City, Rev. B. J. Mulligan, and Revs. J. S. Wallace and P. T. Carew. Among his many friends in the Sanctuary were Archbishop Corrigan, Bishop O'Farrell, of Trenton, Monsignor (Cardinal) Farley, then Vicar-General of the New York diocese, and Rev. Edward P. Allen, D.D., President of Mount St. Mary's College, Emmitsburg, at present Bishop of Mobile. The church was crowded with mourners, among them Professor Edwards of Notre Dame University, Richard H. Clarke, Morgan J. O'Brien, Thomas Addis Emmet, Patrick Farrelly, and Hermann Ridder, the proprietor of the *Catholic News*. Mr. Charles Carroll Lee, Vice President of the United States Catholic Historical Society, represented that organization, of which Dr. Shea was President. The chancel choir of St. Francis Xavier's Church, New York City, sang the Mass under the direction of Father Young, S.J. There was no eulogy, at Dr. Shea's request.

Telegrams and letters of condolence came from all parts of the country to the Shea household, offering sympathy, prayers and Masses for the happy repose of the soul of John Gilmary Shea. "You have reason to be proud of such a father" wrote Archbishop Ryan of Philadelphia, to Isabel Shea, "a father whose name will go down to posterity as the Historian of the American Church, and whose personal character was entirely worthy of this title." Bishop Maes of Covington, Kentucky, who always claimed in his humorous way that the mitre had snuffed out in himself a real historian, wrote that Dr. Shea had saved the great past of Catholicism in America from oblivion. To Mrs. Shea, Cardinal Gibbons said: "The loss you have sustained in the death of your husband, is largely shared by the hierarchy of the United States. I had hoped that the Lord would spare him to us till his great work was completed; but we must bow to the inscrutable will of God . . . . It will be a grave problem to discover the man who can complete the great work which he has been prosecuting all these years." Nugent Robinson called Dr. Shea "one of the noblest minded and cleanest hearted men I ever met. He was a *gentleman;* and this means everything. To me he was a good and sincere friend, helping me, when help was both gracious and grateful. I loved Dr. Shea, and shall have him in my heart always." James C.

Pilling wrote from Washington, D. C.: "Among my most pleasant memories will be the aid, advice and counsel given me by Dr. Shea in my earlier labors, and the pleasant encomiums passed upon those of a later day. Why were there not many more like him! Why should they not live always!"

Mrs. Shea did not long survive her distinguished husband. She passed away on November 11, 1897, at Elizabeth, New Jersey, and was buried by his side in St. Mary's Cemetery.

So far as the field of American Catholic history is in question, there has been no one since Dr. Shea's death to take his place or to carry on his work. The fourth volume of his *History* was published by Mrs. Shea in the course of the year (1892), and was dedicated to Father Patrick Corrigan, whose interest in the work and whose generous support had lightened the last three years of Dr. Shea's life. These years were indeed the only ones in the long stretch from 1852, when his heart was entirely free from financial anxiety. No preface was placed in the volume, since he had not had time to write one; and so we miss the intimate insight he usually gives into the problems connected with his researches and labors. The fourth volume covers the period of a phenomenal stride of the Catholic Church in the United States, from the Fifth Provincial Council of Baltimore to the Second Plenary Council (1843-1866). There are thirteen Books, each divided into chapters, following approximately the geographical growth of the Church in this country. As in his other volumes, illustrations abound, and his pages are replete with maps, portraits of bishops and priests, old churches and institutions, and with facsimiles of episcopal seals and signatures, all chosen with that rare judgment and taste which he displays in all his historical writings.

It is not easy to construct an estimate of John Gilmary Shea's historical works. They consist of so many varied aspects of the historical sciences, linguistics, philology, paleography, historical geography and chronology, the ethnology of the American Indians, critical editions of original texts, biographies, treatises on general historical subjects, his biblical studies, his contributions to encyclopedias and periodical reviews, and lastly the crowning work of his pen, his *History of the Catholic Church in the*

United States, that to appreciate with justice the colossal labors of the man, many factors need to be considered.

There was, first of all, the penury which attended him like Dark Care all through his life, except at the very end; a penury which forced him to accept posts for which, indeed, he was eminently fitted, but in which his great energies were wasted.

One of his last experiences of this nature was with a prominent Catholic publishing house of New York, who had engaged Dr. Shea to write a *History of the United States* for the elementary schools. The correspondence which passed between this firm and Dr. Shea reveals his inability to put into his narrative as facts, legends and anecdotes which historical scholarship had rejected. The volume was completed by another writer.

There was the almost unbelievable accumulation of correspondence imposed on him by reason of the very prominence his historical work had won for him. Those who knew his home life have said that these demands alone would have taxed the full time and far more than the patience of the average man, but which urbanity and courtesy would never allow him to neglect. Even when Father Carroll broke the news to him that his end was quickly approaching, he propped himself up in bed in order to answer five letters of inquiry on historical subjects which had come that morning. One characteristic example of his generous way of answering inquiries is the following letter, written a month before his death to Father Edward J. Schmitt, who was searching for the Bruté Mss.:

"I forward Volumes II and III, and before the end of the month will send Vol. IV. It has been a hard struggle to complete it and see it through the press, as my health is wretched; constant pain, sleeplessness and increasing weakness make literary labor very difficult.

"Bishop Hughes had a great esteem for Rev. Mr. Bruté and apparently very little for the Rev. Mr. Dubois, in his Emmitsburg days. He had an idea of writing a life of Bishop Bruté, and the papers were sent to him. As he was not a man of research or study, he did nothing. I asked his permission to examine them, but he refused although he sent the trunk or trunks to Mr. De Courcy. Bishop Bayley used his recollections of the French Revolution and took the papers to Seton Hall

College.   Some were given away, some lost, and many perished
at a fire.   It was only a remnant that went to Dom Jansion.
I learned later that this clergyman died of a contagious disease,
and that after his death the papers in his room, including what
he had selected from Bishop Bruté's papers, were burned.

"The Abbé Charles Bruté de Remur published in 1887 *Vie de
Mgr. Bruté de Remur* (Rennes, Philhon & Herve publishers).
He seems to have no documents and says he bases his work on
an abridgment of Bishop Bayley's book by Lady Herbert of Lea.
He never had Bishop Bayley's book. He used the books on the
Sisters of Providence, Barberey's *Life of Mrs. Seton,* and letters
of the Lamennais brothers (the good and the bad), which Mr.
De Courcy printed in a French periodical.

"He speaks of the archives of St. Sulpice but apparently did
not glean much, and letters in the possession of a Community of
Brothers founded by De Lamennais.

"Now what material have we?   He was a great letter writer,
and writer of notes, often hasty and incorrect.   Professor Edwards of Notre Dame must have many letters of his.   I have a
few, and others are scattered.   His life at Mount St. Mary's
seems most vague, and yet there was his great good accomplished.   Miss Mary M. Meline went to Mt. St. Mary's and did
some work on a history of that institution.   She may help you.

"For his period as a bishop there is a series of contributions
signed *Vincennes* in the volumes of the *United States Catholic
Miscellany,* which are evidently and clearly his and have never
been used by any writer about him.

"In his hasty way he misled Judge Law in regard to the first
settlement of Vincennes, confounding a tanning venture at the
mouth of the Ohio with Vincennes.   I was very sorry to see this
historical error dressed up in most fantastic guise in the Indiana-
polis Catholic paper, with intrinsic absurdities, making an
expedition from Detroit accompanied by a Jesuit priest, when
there were none at Detroit, and Cadillac hated them too heartily
to have one there.

"When I am free from my volume, and can rest I will see
what I have that may help you.   But I feel that my days, especially my working days are numbered.   Pray for me."

There was more besides the daily calls upon his time and
energy; there was above all the apathy of the Catholics in the
United States, high and low, regarding the preservation of their
past history.   His experience with the United States Catholic
Historical Society of New York City would have forever damp-
ened the enthusiasm of any other man; and it was only when
those outside the Church, Sparks, Bancroft, Parkman and others,
who bore witness to his scrupulous fairness and impartiality,
called attention to the great work he was accomplishing in his
field, that any recognition worthy of the name was given to Dr.
Shea by those of the household of the Faith.

The great Church in whose honor and for whose glory he had
labored never adequately requited him.   What he accomplished
was done in spite of all these and other hindrances that had best,
probably, be passed over silently.

With these facts in mind, one comes to an examination of his
works with less surety of being able to accord them a just critical
analysis.   All concede that as a history, his *History of the Church
in the United States* can never be superseded.   All who write
within that field must come to his volumes as to the principal
source of their researches.   His scholarship is evident on every
page.   His style is persuasive, even eloquent; and there is an
earnestness about his treatment of every point under consideration which leaves no room for doubt as to his irreproachable
sincerity and zeal for the truth.   No one has ever called into
question Dr. Shea's impartiality.   One of his friends said shortly
after his death: "He was always the careful, conscientious historian, setting down naught in malice or bitterness.   He searched
for the truth, and having found it, declared it fearlessly.   Now
that he is gone from us, the wealth of his learning and the importance of his labors will be recalled with wonder and
admiration."

On one point, and one alone, Dr. Shea's sense of fairness has
been questioned at times: his admiration for the work of the
Society of Jesus in this country.   "He was one of us," one of
the Jesuits in New York wrote at the time of his passing.   The
summer before he died, he had arranged, as President of the
United States Catholic Historical Society, to lead its members
in a pilgrimage to the Shrine of Our Lady of Martyrs at Auries-

ville, where all were to receive Holy Communion and to offer up
their prayers for the canonization of the Jesuit Martyrs. Acts of
this nature, even in certain Catholic centers, were apt to be mis-
interpreted. Even the purchase of his great collection of thirty
thousand documents and books by the Jesuits for the Georgetown
Archives and library has been misjudged; and were he to have
lived long enough to have heard such a statement, he would have
been forced to humiliate himself in the one characteristic of his
life wherein he was most sensitive, by confessing to the poverty
which brought the old friends of his youth to his side, with a
generous arrangement that helped him to face death more calmly.
Strange as it may seem, the collection which came to Georgetown
was not the first he was obliged to sell. Twice before, in times
of stress, he had been forced to part with the library he had
gathered, in order to preserve intact from the outside world the
secret of the grinding poverty that encompassed him.

Dr. Shea's contacts with the Society of Jesus were not many.
There were, of course, his six years as a scholastic in the Society
at Fordham and in Montreal (1848-1852). There was Father
Felix Martin's influence upon his vocation of historian; but
Father Martin had returned to France in 1862. Two Jesuit institutions had honored him: one at the beginning of his career.
the other at the end. In the hundreds of names he mentions as
patrons of his *History,* there are not twenty Jesuits. By the
time he came, in the full maturity of study and research, to compose the *History,* all the Fathers of the Society he had known
in his youth had passed away. He was under no obligations to
the Jesuits; in fact, the first two volumes of the *History,* in which
he is said to show partiality to the Society, were through the
press and published before their aid came to him. And what is all
the more vital in any adequate judgment of his impartiality is that
other scholars since his day who have worked independently
among the same sources have reached his conclusions, and have
accepted them as correct. Not that Dr. Shea's volumes are free
from blunders. In some cases there are serious historical blunders
which were partly unavoidable because all the source-material
was not then available. But, viewing the wide range of his historical labors and especially the all-important fact that he
practically had to pioneer his way into archives and libraries all

over the world for the sources he used, there is none to deny his accurate erudition, his unfailing objectivity, his cautious and prudent statements of the truth as he found it.

It is not in this aspect of his work that objections need be made against Dr. Shea, but in another, though less serious, phase of his scholarship. With the exception of the *Catholic Missions,* and the *Life of Archbishop Carroll,* Dr. Shea's historical volumes are lacking in symmetry. The first, third, and fourth volumes of the *History of the Church in the United States,* while well written, are constructed in an unsatisfactory way. The order of time is naturally kept in each section and chapter and book of these volumes, but the arrangement of each volume leaves much to be desired. Dr. Shea was not able to solve a problem which yet remains to be answered: how to treat in a systematic fashion geographical units that will stand apart ecclesiastically in spite of all identities and similarities.

Some day, perhaps, a new edition of the *History* will be attempted in order to bring the narrative down to within recent times, and it may then be found advisable to re-arrange all the material presented in the four volumes in a more logical and concise fashion. In this way, the repetitions in Dr. Shea's *History* will be avoided; the growth of Catholicism, especially after 1815, will assume a more logical presentation; and the social and political factors of our national life influencing that growth will not remain, as they now are, subdued in his pages.

Like all pioneers, Dr. Shea must wait a still longer time before the inherent worth of his labors is given the national recognition it deserves. His fellow-Catholics have not altogether failed in this posthumous honoring of their great historian and it is the pleasant duty of this chronicle to record the action taken by the Knights of Columbus, of Newark, N. J., who chose October 12, 1912, as the day to commemorate the Father of American Catholic History. A handsome bronze tablet had been placed in St. Patrick's Cathedral, Newark, with this inscription:

IN MEMORY OF
JOHN GILMARY SHEA
HISTORIAN OF THE CATHOLIC CHURCH
IN THE UNITED STATES

BORN 1824   DIED 1892

FAITHFUL TO TRUTH AS AN HISTORIAN, ABLE
AND FEARLESS AS AN EDITOR, ZEALOUS AND
DEVOTED AS A CATHOLIC, PATRIOTIC
AS A CITIZEN

The tablet was unveiled on that afternoon by his daughter, Emma Isabel Shea, in the presence of the Bishops of Newark and Trenton, and of a great gathering of Dr. Shea's friends and admirers. The principal address was given by Dr. James J. Walsh, K. S. G., himself an indefatigable laborer in the field of Catholic history and apologetics. "About 1889 or 1890," Dr. Walsh said, "I had the privilege of meeting the man whom we are assembled to honor today under circumstances that gave me an opportunity to learn something of his character, and to recognize something of the value of the work that he was doing. I was a young teacher at the time, and I remember now a little amusedly how much I was mistaken in my estimate of the man. I was inclined to think him one of those rather impractical individuals, who, finding the ordinary ways of men difficult, had withdrawn into a life of books mainly so as to be able to avoid the hurry and bustle and the unceasing demands of the world around him. I had no idea at all of the vocational side of Mr. Shea's wonderful work and of the scholarship that it both called into play and developed, and of the magnificent memorial to his own intellectual patience and love for truth and to our pioneer Catholics here in America that he was raising. I knew that his histories represented an enormous amount of research, under the most difficult circumstances, but I had no idea that Mr. Shea was raising for himself a monument more lasting than bronze, one that will keep his name in memory among the scholars of this country when the vast majority of the practical men who have devoted themselves to business and made money will be forgotten. I suppose one has to be nearly a generation older than I was then properly to appreciate the work of such a scholar and a historical investigator.

DR. SHEA'S GRAVE

KNIGHTS OF COLUMBUS MEMORIAL TABLET IN THE
CATHEDRAL, NEWARK, N. J.

"After this act of reparation to his memory, which I feel due to him, I may try to tell you a little of what he did accomplish and of what it came to mean for the intellectual life of this country. It is more due to John Gilmary Shea than to any other that we have the precious records of the missionaries of the early generations of Catholics in this country; that we know what Catholics in the Revolution did to secure for us our precious heritage and liberty; besides all that he brought together with regard to the early days of Church organization here. The lives of our first great Catholic Bishop and his earliest successors; the career of our first great Catholic University, Georgetown; the history of the Councils of the Church here in America, those magnificent assemblages that knew so well how to weigh and duly consider the spiritual and religious needs of this country, all these were illuminated by the patient work, the careful investigation, but, above all, by what I may call, the historical genius of John Gilmary Shea. For the historical writer, like the poet, is born, not made. Only native genius enables a man to do it as Shea did it.

"Unfortunately, there is another aspect of the writing question in which the historical writer resembles the poet only too often. Some one said not long since that the poet is born, but not paid. The historical writer, especially who treats serious subjects seriously, is likely to find that his works sell quite as little as the poet's, but yet that he must make a living. In the face of this obstacle, which usually turns most men aside from devotion to the intellectual life for its own sake, John Gilmary Shea continued to devote himself to historical writing, caring little for the rewards, yet succeeding in a very practical way in making a living and having that happiness which comes to a man who is doing the work that he cares to do. After all there is no happiness except that. Blessed is the man who has found his work, and John Gilmary Shea had surely found his."

This act of gratitude atoned in a measure for the tardiness the Church in the United States had shown in recognizing the eminent merit of its most distinguished layman. In one of the keenest estimates of John Gilmary Shea, we are told that "the Catholic Church in America owes him a debt that can never be substantially repaid. It never had a more painstaking searcher after truth, never a more devoted lover of the truth, never a more unselfish, self-sacrificing son than the modest and retiring scholar who worked for many years in her service at a pittance that was barely enough to keep body and soul together in the patient task of disseminating a knowledge of the work of the Church in the United States, and arousing an interest in that work wherever the English language was spoken."

A generation of students and writers in the field of American Catholic history has grown up since the death of John Gilmary Shea. Many of these have been satisfied to repeat in their own way the brilliant pages he contributed to the story of our Catholic past. Few have approached Shea in his genius for historical research or in his ability to bring to light the scattered sources of our history. None have equalled him in devotion to the cause of American Catholic history, and he stands, today, as he did when death called him in 1892, the leader in his chosen vocation. That he accomplished an uncommonly large amount of historical work is evidenced by the bibliography of his writings appended to these pages. No one knew so well as he the equally large amount of research and study he was forced to leave undone. His eyes were ever upon the generation which was to follow him, but the wish, so often spoken to those about him that American Catholic scholarship would furnish the student and writer who would carry on the work after he was gone, has not yet been fulfilled. In Shea's life, in the recital of the many difficulties amid which he carried on his great work, in the tragic poverty that was ever present all through his years almost until the end, and in the unselfish and uncomplaining way he worked out his self-appointed task, the aspirants of our day have an exemplar unique in the annals of lay apostleship. Wherever his memory is cherished as one who gave of his rich and mature scholarship to the Catholic Church in the United States, there will his zeal find an emulation; and his example a worthy following.

BIBLIOGRAPHY OF SHEA'S WORKS

In one of Shea's note-books there is an incomplete bibliographical list of his historical writings, drawn up probably in 1888. The number of works given is one hundred and thirty-seven. Seventy-four of these are original compositions and sixty-three are works which Shea edited. To this number should be added the thirty-two volumes of the *Catholic Directory* which he edited from 1858 to 1890. The *Bibliography of John Gilmary Shea*, published by Rev. Edward Spillane, S. J., after Shea's death, in HISTORICAL RECORDS AND STUDIES, December, 1912, contains 247 titles, ranging from short historical sketches to works on general and special topics, reprints of historical documents, devotional works, and publications of original sources. The prodigious activity of Dr. Shea is unique in American historiography. There is no doubt that many unsigned articles exist which would add considerably to the complete bibliography of his works.

I. PUBLICATION OF SOURCES

Narrative of a Captivity Among the Mohawk Indians and a description of New Netherland in 1642-43, by Father Isaac Jogues, S. J. With Memoir of the Holy Missionary, 8vo., pp. 69. New York 1856; second edition, 1857.

Perils of the Ocean and Wilderness; or, Narratives of Shipwrecks and Indian Captivities. Gleaned from the early Missionary Annals. 12 mo., pp. 206. 1856; second edition, 1857.

Journal of an Embassy from Canada to the United Colonies of New England, in 1650. By Father Gabriel Druillettes of the Society of Jesus. Translated from the original manuscript with notes. New York, 1857.

Gravier (J.), *Relation de la Mission des Illinois* (1693), pp. 65. 1857. (Cramoisy, No. 1).

Bigot (J.), *Relation de la Mission Abanaquaise* (1684), pp. 61. 1857. (Cramoisy, No. 2).

Bigot, (J.), *Relation de la Mission Abanaquaise* (1685), pp. 21. 1858. (Cramoisy, No. 3).

Bigot, (J.), *Relation de la Mission Abanaquaise* (1701), pp. 34. 1858. (Cramoisy, No. 4).

Cavelier (R.), *Voyage de M. La Salle* (1685, pp. 54. 1858. Cramoisy, No. 5).

Chaumonot (J. M.), *Autobiographie,* pp. 108, 1858, (Cramoisy, Nos. 6-7).

Lettre de P. Bigot à Annexy, pp. 9. 1858. (Cramoisy, No. 23).

Tranchepain (A.), *Voyage des Ursulines à la Nouvelle Orleans,* pp. 62, 1859. (Cramoisy, No. 8). Translation: *Account of the Voyage of the Ursulines to New Orleans in 1727,* in the *United States Catholic Historical Magazine,* Vol. 1 (1888), pp. 28-42.

Registres des Baptesmes et Sepultures au Fort Duquesne, 1753, '54, '55, '56, pp. 51. 1859. (Craimoisy, No. 9).

Journal de la Guerre contres les Chicachas, 1739-40, pp. 92. (Cramoisy, No. 10).

Gravier (J.), *Voyage à l'embouchure du Mississippi, 1700,* pp. 68. 1859. (Cramoisy, No. 11).

Diary of George Washington, from 1789 to 1791. Together with his journal of a tour to the Ohio in 1753. Edited by B. J. Lossing with notes by Shea. 12 mo. pp. 248. New York, 1860.

Dablon (C.), *Relation de la Nouvelle France, 1673-79,* pp. 290. 1860. (Cramoisy, No. 12).

Relations diverses sur la bataille du Malenguele, pp. 75. 1860. (Cramoisy, No. 14).

Gendron. *Quelques Particularitez sur le Pays des Hurons,* pp. 26. 1860. (Cramoisy, No. 25).

A Relation of the Discovery of the South Sea Made by the Rivers of New France. Sent from Quebec by Father Dablon, Superior General of the missions of the Society of Jesus, August 1, 1674. In the *Historical Magazine,* August, 1861.

Early Voyages Up and Down the Mississippi, by Cavelier, St. Cosme, Le Suer, Gravier, and Guignas, with an introduction and notes, pp. 191. Albany, 1861.

Dablon (C.), *Relation de la Nouvelle France, 1672-73,* pp. 219. 1861. (Cramoisy, No. 13).

Relation des Missions du Seminaire de Quebec, 1700, pp. 66. 1861. (Cramoisy, No. 15).

A Description of the Province and City of New York, with plans of the city and several forts as they existed in the year 1695, by John Miller. A new edition with an introduction and copious historical notes by J. G. Shea. 8vo. pp. 127. New York, 1862.

Jogues (I,), *Novum Belgium,* pp. 44. 1862. (Cramoisy, No. 16).

Sagean (M.), *Extrait des Voyages de Matthieu Sagean.* pp. 32. 1863. (Cramoisy, No. 17).

Milet, (P.), *Relation d'une captivité parmi les Omneiouts, 1690-91,* pp. 56. 1864. (Cramoisy, No. 18).

Driuillettes (G.), *Epistola ad Joannem Winthrop,* pp. 13. 1864. Cramoisy, No. 24).

Operations of the French Fleet under Count De Grasse, 1781-82, as described in two contemporaneous journals, pp. 216. New York, 1864.

Affairs at Fort Chartres, 1768-81, pp. 12. Albany, 1864.

A Relation of the successful beginnings of the Lord Baltimore's Plantation in Maryland. Being an extract of certain letters written from thence, by some of the adventurers to their friends in England. Anno Domini 1634. Printed by Joel Munsell, September, 1865, from a transcript of the original work in the British Museum. New York, 1865.

Sot-Weed Factor; or a voyage to Maryland. Reprint of London ed., 1708. Albany, 1865.

Relation des Affaires du Canada en 1696, pp. 73. 1865. (Cramoisy, No. 20).

Bigot (J.), *Relation de la Mission Abanaquaise, 1702,* pp. 26. 1865. (Cramoisy, No. 21).

Gravier (J.), *Lettre sur les Affaires de la Louisiana,* pp. 18. Cramoisy, No. 22).

Colden's History of the Five Nations depending on the Province of New York. With an introduction and notes by J. G. S. New York, 1866. (Reprint of the rare New York edition of 1727).

A Character of the Province of Maryland, described in four Distinct Parts. Also a Small Treatise on the wild and naked Indians (or Susquehannokes) of Maryland. Their Customs, Manners, Absurdities and Religion. Together with a collection of Historical Letters by George Alsop. A new edition with an Introduction and Copious Historical and Biographical Notes. Pp. 125. New York 1869. (No. 5 of Gowan's *Bibliotheca Americana*). Another edition, Baltimore, 1880.

Daniel Hyacinth Mary Lienard de Beaujeu, Commandant of Fort Duquesne and of the French Forces in the Battle of July 9, 1755. In the *Penna. Magazine of History,* Vol. 8 (1884), p. 121.

Réné Goupil, Captain and Martyr. (Trans. from Jogues papers, 1856), in the *Messenger of the Sacred Heart,* for March, 1885.

Notes on the Two Jesuit Manuscripts belonging to the estate of the late Hon. John Neilson of Quebec, Canada, by l'Abbé Sasseville and Dr. John Gilmary Shea. Edited by George M. Fairchild. Pp. 16. Printed privately, New York, 1887. (Cf. *United States Catholic Historical Magazine,* vol. 1, p. 534, New York, 1887).

Chauchetière. *La Vie de la B. Catherine Tegahkouita, dictée à present la Sainte Sauvagesse.* Pp. 179. New York, 1887. (Cramoisy, No. 25).

Statutes of the Diocese of Louisiana and the Floridas, issued by the Rt. Rev. Luis Peñalver y Cardenas, 1795. Pp. 29. New York, 1887. Reprint from *United States Cath. Hist. Mag.,* October, 1887.

Statutes relating to Florida. .By Rt. Rev. J. G. de Palacios. (Diocesan Synod convened at Havana, 1684). Pp. 13. Reprint from *United States Cath. Hist. Mag.,* July, 1887.

Captivity of Father Peter Millet, S. J., among the Oneida Indians. His own narrative, with supplementary documents. New York, 1887. (Translation of No. 18 of the Cramoisys). *the Rt. Rev. Luis Peñalver y Cardenas, 1795.* Pp. 29. New York, 1889. Reprint from *United States Cath. Hist. Mag.,* July, 1888.

An Address from the Roman Catholics of America to George Washington, Esq., President of the United States. (London, 1790). Pp. 11, N.p. n.d. (Reprint with portraits of Washington, Archbishop Carroll, facsimile of the manuscript of Washington's answer, and Shea's notes on the Catholic signers).

2. American Linguistics

(*Grammars and Dictionaries of Indian Languages*)

Shea, J. G. *A French-Onondaga Dictionary, from a manuscript of the seventeenth century.* Pp. 103. New York, 1860.

Mengarini, Gregory. *A Selish or Flathead Grammar.* Pp. viii-122. New York, 1861.

Smith, Buckingham. *A Grammatical Sketch of the Heve Language translated from an unpublished Spanish manuscript.* Pp. 26. New York, 1861.

Arroyo De La Cuesta, Felipe. *Grammar of the Mutsun Language, spoken at the mission of San Juan Bautista, Alta California.* Pp. viii-48. New York, 1861.

Smith, Buckingham. *Grammar of the Pima or Vevome, a language of Sonora, from a manuscript of the eighteenth century.* Pp. viii-97. New York, 1862.

Doctrina Christiana y Confesionario en Lengua Nevome, Sea La Pima, propria de Sonora. Pp. 32. New York, 1862.

Pandosy. *Grammar and Dictionary of the Yakama Language.* Pp. viii-97. New York, 1862.

Sitjar, Bonaventure. *Vocabulary of the Language of San Antonio Mission, California.* Pp. xix-53. New York, 1861.

Arroyo De La Guesta, Felipe. *A Vocabulary or Phrase Book of the Mutsun Language of Alta California.* Pp. VIII-96. New York, 1862.

Maillard, Abbé. *Grammar of the Mikmaque Language of Nova Scotia, edited from manuscripts by Rev. Joseph M. Bellinger.* Pp. 101. New York, 1864.

Bruyas, James. *Radical Words of the Mohawk Language, with their derivatives.* Pp. 123. New York, 1862.

Gibbs, George. *Alphabetical Vocabularies of the Clallam and Lummi.* Pp. viii-40. New York, 1863.

Gibbs, George. *A Dictionary of the Cinook Jargon, or, Trade Language of Oregon.* Pp. xiv-43. New York, 1863.

Gibbs, George. *Alphabetical Vocabulary of the Chinook Language.* Pp. xviii-23. New York, 1863.

Matthews, Washington. *Grammar and Dictionary of the Language of the Hidatsa (Minnetarees, Grosventres of the Missouri), with an introductory sketch of the tribe.* Pp. xxv-148. New York, 1873.

Matthews, Washington. *Hisatsa (Minnetaree) English Dictionary.* Pp. 149-168. New York, 1874.

3. TRANSLATIONS

*The Catholic Church in the United States: A Sketch of its ec-
clesiastical History,* by Henry De Courcy, translated and enlarged by J. G. Shea. Pp. 591. New York, 1856; 2d ed., New
York, 1857.

The Saints of Erin; Legendary History of Ireland, translated
from the French of Tachet De Barneval. Pp. 308. Boston,
1857.

History and General Description of New France, translated from
the French of Charlevoix. 6 vols., New York, 1866-72. (A
second edition with a biographical sketch of Dr. Shea was published in New York, 1901).

Hennepin's Description of Louisiana. Pp. 407. Map. New
York, 1880. (Translated from the edition of 1683).

First Establishment of the Faith in New France, translated from
the French of Le Clercq. 2 vols., New York, 1881.

*The Expedition of Don Diego Dionisio de Peñalosa from Santa
Fé to the River Meschipi and Quivira in 1662, as described by
Father Nicholas de Freytas; with an account of Peñalosa's pro-
jects to aid the French to conquer the mining country in
Northern Mexico; and his connection with Cavelier de la Salle.*
Pp. 101. New York, 1882.

4. GENERAL HISTORY

*First Book of History; Combined with Geography and Chron-
ology, for younger classes.* Pp. 254. New York, 1854.

*A General History of Modern Europe, from the beginning of the
Sixteenth Century to the Restoration of the Empire in France
in 1853.* Pp. 485. New York, 1854. Third revised edition,
1870.

Is Froude a Historian? in the *American Catholic Quarterly Review,* for January, 1880.

5. AMERICAN HISTORY

*Discovery and Exploration of the Mississippi Valley, with the
Original Narratives of Marquette, Membré, Hennepin, and
Anastase Douay, wtih a facsimile of the newly discovered map
of Marquette, and facsimile of the letter of Allouez.* Pp.
lxxx-257. New York, 1852.

A School History of the United States from the Earliest Period to the Present Time. Pp. 288. New York, 1855.

Cathechism of the History of the United States. Pp. 180. New York, 1855.

An Elementary History of the United States. Pp. 157. New York, 1855.

The Life and Character of Garakonthie, Sachem of Onondago. Address before the New York Historical Society, October 2, 1855.

The Indian Tribes of Wisconsin, in the *Wisconsin Historical Society Collections,* Vol. 3, (1856), p. 125-138.

The Identity of the Andastes, Minquas, Susquehannas, and Conestogues, in the *Historical Magazine,* Vol. 2 (1858), pp. 294-296.

Chicago from 1673 to 1725, or What is Known of the First Half Century of its History, in the *Historical Magazine,* Vol. 5 (1861), pp. 222-227.

Micmac or Recollect Hieroglyphics in the *Historical Magazine,* Vol. 5, pp. 289-292.

Christopher Columbus and Beatrice Enriques. A defence of Columbus, in the *Historical Magazine,* Vol. 5 (1861), pp. 393-399.

An Historical Sketch of the Tiononntates or Dinondadies now called Wyandots, in the *Historical Magazine,* Vol. 5 (1861), pp. 403-409.

Fallen Brave: .A Biographical Memorial of the American Officers who have given their lives for the preservation of tha Union. Pp. 224. New York, 1861 (One volume was all that was published).

The New York Negro Plot of 1741-2, paper read before the New York Historical Society, May 6, 1862.

Of What Nation were the Inhabitants of Stadacona and Hochelaga at the Time of Cartier's Voyage?, in the *Historical Magazine,* Vol. 9 (1865), pp. 144-145.

Indian Names (of geographical features), in the Mohawk Language, in the *Historical Magazine,* Vol. 10 (1866), p. 58.

A Child's History of the United States. 3 vols. Pp. 512, 447, 443, New York, 1872. Second edition, 1886.

The First Attempt to Settle Virginia, paper read before the New York Historical Society, October 1, 1872.

Discovery of the Mississippi River, in the *Wisconsin Historical Society Collections,* Vol. 7, (1876), p. 111.

What the United States Owes to James II, in the *American Catholic Quarterly Review,* for April, 1877.

The Blue Laws of Connecticut, in the *American Catholic Quarterly Review,* for July, 1877.

Address Delivered Before the Missouri Historical Society (at St. Louis) July 19, 1878, the anniversary of the discovery of the Mississippi by Marquette and Joliet, pp. 20. New York, 1878.

The Rapid Increase of the Dangerous Classes in the United States, in the *American Catholic Quarterly Review,* for April 1879.

The Canadian Element in the United States, in the *American Catholic Quarterly Review,* for October, 1879.

Early Chapters of Cayuga History: Jesuit Missions in Goi-o-gouen, 1656-34. *Also an account of the Sulpician Mission among the emigrant Cayuagas, about Quinte Bay, 1668.* By Charles Hawley, D. D., with an introduction by Shea. Auburn, 1879.

Bursting of Pierre Margry's La Salle Bubble, pp. 24. New York, 1879.

What Right Has the Federal Government to Mismanage the Indians?, in the *American Catholic Quarterly Review,* for July, 1881.

The Lesson of President Garfield's Assassination, in the *American Catholic Quarterly Review,* for October, 1881.

Where Are the Remains of Christopher Columbus,? read before the New York Historical Society, Nov. 7, 1882. Printed in the *Magazine of American History,* Vol. 9, (1883), pp. 1-18.

Bancroft's "History of the United States," in the *American Catholic Quarterly Review,* for October, 1883.

Puritanism in New England, in the *American Catholic Quarterly Review,* for January, 1884.

Columbus and the Men of Palos, read before the New York Historical Society, April 1, 1884. Printed in the *United States Catholic Historical Magazine,* for April, 1888.

Maryland and the Controversies as to her Early History, in the *American Catholic Quarterly Review,* for October 1885.

Beaujeu and Fort Du Quesne, in the *Magazine of American History,* Vol. 16 (1886), p. 586.

The Boston of Winthrop, in the *American Catholic Quarterly Review,* for April, 1887.

The First Epic of Our Country, by the Poet Conquistador of New Mexico, Captain Gaspar de Villagra, pp. 16. Reprint from *United States Catholic Historical Magazine,* April, 1887.

Pope's Day in New England and Other Places, pp. 7. New York, 188.

Federal Schemes to Aid Common Schools in the Southern States, in the *American Catholic Quarterly Review,* for April, 1888.

Why is Canada not a Part of the United States?, pp. 15. Reprint from the *United States Catholic Historical Magazine,* April, 1889.

The Columbus Centenary of 1892, in the *American Catholic Quarterly Review,* October, 1889.

Discovery and Exploration of the Mississippi Valley, pp. 49. New York, 1890.

Illinois, Osage, and Otoptata Chiefs in Paris in 1725, pp. 7. New York, 1890.

The Bible in American History, in the *American Catholic Quarterly Review,* January, 1898.

History of the United States. In a compilation entitled *The Cross and the Flag, Our Church and Country. Heroic deeds for the old Faith and the New Land, from the discovery of America to the dawn of the Twentieth Century. Comprising a full, true and strictly impartial history of the United States.* Shea's contribution is from p. 107 to p. 398. New York, 1899.

Dongan's Charter of the City of New York, pp. 10. Reprint from *United States Catholic Historical Magazine,* July, 1889.

Shea's contributions to Appleton's *American Cyclopedia* (1874-82) consist of over one hundred articles on the North American Indian tribes and their customs and on prominent explorers of the Indian country. To these should be added the chapters on *Ancient Florida, and Jesuits, Recollects, and the Indians,* in Winsor's *Narrative and Critical History of America.* In the second edition of Duyckinck's *Cyclopedia of American Literature* (1886) there is an article by Shea on *The Literature of New France and Canada.*

6. AMERICAN CATHOLIC HISTORY

History of the Catholic Missions Among the Indian Tribes of the United States, 1529-1854.   Pp. 514.   New York, 1854. Other editions, 1855, 1857, 1858 (German), 1870, 1882, 1899.

General Catholic Directory, Almanac and Ordo for the year of Our Lord.   Edited by Dr. Shea from 1858 to 1890.

The Capuchin Missions in Maine, in the *Historical Magazine,* Vol. 8, (1860), pp. 177, 301.

Notes on the Early History of the Catholic Church in New England, in the *Historical Magazine,* Vol. 5 (1869), pp. 313, 39.

Early Missions in Acadia, in the *Catholic World,* for February and March, 1871.

The Log Chapel on the Rappahannock. Erected A. D. 1570—The First Christian Shrine in the Old Dominion, in the *Catholic World,* for March, 1875.

The Catholic Church in American History, in the *American Catholic Quarterly Review,* for January, 1876.

Romance and Reality of the Death of Father James Marquette, and the Recent Discovery of His Remains, in the *Catholic World,* for November, 1877.

The Catholic Church of New York City, with Sketches of their History and Lives of the Present Pastors. With an Introduction on the Early History of Catholicity on the Island, and, Lives of the Most Rev. Archbishops and Bishops, pp. 748. New York, 1878.

The Catholic Church in the United States, in the Recent Translation of Alzog, in the *American Catholic Quarterly Review,* for January, 1879.

History of the Catholic Church in the United States. From the Earliest Settlement of the Country to the Present Time. With Biographical Sketches, Accounts of Religious Orders, Councils. Pp. 701, New York, 1879.   A revised and augmented edition of the earlier work by De Courcy and Shea, (1856).

Christ in His Church. A Catholic Church History.   Translated from the original of Rev. L. C. Businger, by Rev. Richard Brennan, LL.D., together with a History of the Church in

America by John Gilmary Shea, LL.D. Pp. X-426. Shea's sketch of American Church history is from p. 313 to p. 426. New York, 1881.

The Anti-Catholic Issue in the Late Election; the Relation of, Catholics to the Political Parties, in the *American Catholic Quarterly Review,* for January, 1881.

The Earliest Discussions of the Catholic Question in New England—Segenot and Burett, 1727, in the *American Catholic Quarterly Review,* for April, 1881.

The Early Franciscan Missions in this Country, in the *American Catholic Quarterly Review,* for January, 1882.

The Religious Rights of Catholics in Public Institutions, in the *American Catholic Quarterly Review,* for April, 1882.

Early Catholicity in Indiana, in the *Catholic World,* for April, 1882.

The American Hierarchy in its Three-fold Source: Three Representative Bishops, in the *American Catholic Quarterly Review,* for April, 1883.

Converts: Their Influence and Work in this Country, ibid., July, 1883.

The Coming Plenary Council of Baltimore, ibid., April, 1884.

The Progress of the Church in the United States, from the First Provincial Council to the Third Plenary Council of Baltimore, ibid., July, 1884.

Catholic Free Schools in the United States: Their Necessity, Condition, and Future, ibid., October, 1884.

The Pastoral of the Third Plenary Council of Baltimore, ibid., January, 1885.

The Proposed American Catholic University, ibid., April, 1885.

The Inauguration of the Temporary Chapel at Auriesville, N. Y., ibid., October, 1885.

Catholics of the United States during the Revolution, in *Donahue's Magazine,* for August, 1885 (An address delivered before the U. S. Catholic Historical Society, May 14, 1885).

The Feast of the Assumption at the Shrine of Our Lady of Martyrs. A Glorious Spectacle, in the *Catholic World,* August, 1885.

A History of the Catholic Church within the Limits of the United

States, from the first attempted colonization to the present time.
4 vols. 1886-92.

(1) *Catholic Church in Colonial Days. The Thirteen Colonies
—The Ottawa and Illinois Country—Louisiana—Florida
—Texas—New Mexico and Arizona. 1521-1763.* Pp.
663. 1886.

(2) *Life and Times of the Most Rev. John Carroll, Bishop and
First Archbishop of Baltimore. Embracing the History
of the Catholic Church in the United States, 1763-1815.*
Pp. 695. 1888.

(3) *History of the Catholic Church in the United States from
the Division of the Diocese of Baltimore, 1808, and death
of Archbishop Carroll, 1815, to the fifth Provincial Council of Baltimore, 1843.* Pp. 732. 1890.

(4) *History of the Catholic Church in the United States from
the Fifth Provincial Council of Baltimore, 1843, to the
Second Plenary Council of Baltimore, 1866.* Pp. 727.
1892.

No Actual Need of a Catholic Party in the United States, in
the *American Catholic Quarterly Review,* for October, 1887.

A Century of Catholicity in the United States, in the *Catholic
World,* for November, 1889.

Bostonian Ignorance of Catholic Doctrine, in the *American Catholic Quarterly Review,* for January, 1889.

The Jesuit Estates in Canada, ibid., April, 1889.

Jansenists, Old Catholics, and their Friends in America, ibid.,
July, 1889.

*Consecration of the Philadelphia Cathedral, Historical Reminis-
cences, ibid.,* July, 1890.

*An Appeal in Behalf of the United States Catholic Historical
Society,* pp. 8. Elizabeth, N. J., 1891.

*Memorial of the First Centenary of Georgetown College, D. C.,
Comprising a history of Georgetown University by John Gilmary Shea, LL.D., and an account of the Centennial Celebration of the Faculty.* Pp. xv-480. New York, 1891.

*The Defenders of Our Faith: Their Devotion to the Church.
Biographies and portraits of Our Cardinals, Archbishops, and
Bishops, setting forth their zeal and labor in the development
of Faith and Morals. Including an explanation of the doc-*

trines of the Church. A full account of the Plenary Council of Baltimore; The Church in its History, Teachings, Trials and Triumphs in America, pp. 678. New York, 1892.

Catholic Gems or Treasures of the Church. A Repository of Catholic Instruction and Devotion, by the Very Rev. Francis De Ligney, S. J., and John Gilmary Shea, LL.D. A Biographical Portrait Gallery of the Most Rev. Archbishops and Bishops of the Catholic Church in the United States and Canada, together with portraits and biographical notes of many other eminent prelates. (101 Portraits). New York, 1893.

World's Columbian Catholic Congress, 1893, pp. 208. Chicago, 1893.

Martyr Memories of America. An unpublished Ms. by the late J. G. Shea, in the *Ave Maria,* July 20; October 26, 1895; September 5; October 24, 1896; November 6; December 18, 1897.

Sir John James of Crishall, Essex. Bart. The Benefactor of the Pennsylvania Missions, pp. 7, N.d.n.p. Reprinted in the *United States Catholic Historical Magazine,* January, 1888.

General Description of the Metropolitan Province of Baltimore in the United States of America, pp. 4. N.p.n.d.

Illinois and Miami Vocabulary and Lord's Prayer, pp. 9. N.p.n.d.

Holy Personages of Canada and the United States, Whose Canonization is Begun. Ven. Isaac Jogues, S.J., Ven. René Goupil, S. J., Ven. Maria de Agreda, O. S. F., Ven. Mary of the Incarnation, Ursuline (1672), Ven. Margaret of Bourgeoys, (1700), Ven. Francis de Laval de Montmorency (1708), Anthony Margil of Jesus, O. S. F. (1726), Ven. Mary Margaret Dufrost de Lajemmerais (1771).

Jesuits, Recollects, and the Indians, in the *Wisconsin Historical Society Collections,* Vol. 4, pp. 236-298.

Spanish Mission Colony on the Rappahannock: the First European Settlement in Virginia. Pp. 11. W. W. Beach. *Indian Miscellany,* p. 333.

7. LIVES

Life of St. Angela Merici of Brescia: Foundress of the Order of St. Ursula. With an account of the Order in Ireland, Canada, and the United States. Translated from the French of Canon Parenty. Pp. 251. Philadelphia, 1857. Second edition, 1859.

The Lincoln Memorial. A Record of the life, assassination and obsequies of the martyred President. Pp. 288. New York, 1865.

A Bad Beginning for a Saint, or the Early Life of Father Chaumonot, in the *Catholic World,* for August, 1872.

Memoir of Buckingham Smith in the Appendix to the latter's *Narrative of Alva Nuñez Cabeza de Vaca.* New York, 1873.

The Life of Pope Pius IX and the great events in the history of the Church during His Pontificate. Pp. 440. New York, 1877.

A Pioneer of the West, Rev. Charles Nerinckx, in the *American Catholic Quarterly Review,* for July, 1880.

Obituary Notice of Edmund Bailey O'Callaghan, in the *Magazine of American History,* Vol. 5 (1880), pp. 77-81.

The Ven. Anthony Margil of Jesus, of the Order of St. Francis, Apostle of Texas and Guatemala, in the *Catholic World* for February, 1885.

Life of Father Jogues, Missionary Priest of the Society of Jesus. Slain by the Mohawk Iroquois in the present State of New York, October 18, 1646. By Father Felix Martin, S. J. With Father Jogues' account of the captivity and death of his companion, René Goupil, slain September 29, 1642. From the French, with a portrait and a map of the Mohawk Country by Gen. John S. Clark. Pp. 263. New York, 1885. Revised edition, 1886.

Cardinal McCloskey, in *Donahoe's Magazine,* for January, 1886.

The Hierarchy of the Catholic Church in the United States. Embracing sketches of all the Archbishops and Bishops from the establishment of the See of Baltimore to the present time. Also an account of the Plenary Councils of Baltimore, and a brief history of the Church in the United States. Profusely illustrated with portraits, to which are added numerous portraits with brief biographical notes of Canadian Bishops of our own time. Pp. 445. New York, 1886.

Christopher Columbus: This Century's Estimates of His Life and Work, in the *American Catholic Quarterly Review,* for July, 1887.

Pictorial Lives of the Saints with Reflections for every day in the year compiled from "Butler's Lives" and other approved sources. To which are added Lives of the American Saints recently placed on the calendar for the United States by special petition of the Third Plenary Council of Baltimore, and also the Lives of the new saints canonized in 1881 by His Holiness Pope Leo XIII. Pp. 538. New York, 1888. Second edition, 1899.

Archbishop John Hughes, New York, 1889.

Ven. John Nepomucene Neumann, C. SS. R.; Ven. Magin Catala, O. S. F., in the *Ave Maria,* February 1-22, 1890.

The Founder of Our Heirarchy, Bishop Carroll, An Anniversary, in the *Ave Maria,* August 16, 1890.

8. BIBLIOGRAPHIES

A Bibliographical Account of Catholic Bibles, Testaments, and other portions of the Scripture translated from the Latin Vulgate and printed in the United States. Pp. 48. New York, 1859. (Copy in New York Public Library. Photostat copies in library of American Catholic Historical Society (Philadelphia), and in Library of the Catholic University of America, (Washington, D. C.).

Edmund Bailey O'Callaghan's Publications, in the *Pilot* (Boston), for August 7, 1880.

Bibliography of Hennepin's Works, pp. 13. New York, 1880.

An Essay on the Bibliography of the Councils, Synods, Statutes of the Catholic Church in the United States. Pamphlet, pp. 16. New York, 1890.

9. DEVOTIONAL WORKS

Illustrated Novena of St. Francis Xavier of the Society of Jesus, Apostle of the Indies and Japan, and Patron of the propagation of the Faith. With a selection of Prayers. Montreal, 1850.

The Life of the Blessed Virgin Mary, of her Chaste Spouse Saint Joseph, and her holy parents Saint Joachim and Saint Anne. Translated from the *Life of the Blessed Virgin* by Romualdo Gentilucci; the *Life of Saint Joseph* by Father Vallego, a Mexican Jesuit of the seventeenth century; the *Lives Saint Joachim and Saint Anne,* by Father Binet, S. J. New York, 1856.

Seraphic Manual. New York, 1858.

The Method of Meditation. Translated from the Dutch of Rev.

John Roothann, General of the Society of Jesus. Pp. 89, New
York, 1858.

*The Earliest Public Honor to Mary in Northern America.
Jacques Cartier's Pilgrimage and vow to Our Lady of Roca-
madour at Quebec, in 1534,* in the *Catholic World* for October,
1881.

10. MISCELLANEOUS WRITINGS

Changes in Protestant Public Worship, in the *Catholic World,*
for June, 1874.

The Inquisition, in the *American Catholic Quarterly Review,* for
April, 1876.

*What the Church and the Popes Have Done for the Science of
Geography, ibid.,* October, 1878.

*The Jewish Element in the Church a Proof of its Apostolic
Origin, ibid.,* October, 1878.

*A Rehabilitation of Catholic Terms in Dictionaries of the Eng-
lish Language, ibid.,* April, 1880.

Our Great Goddess and Her Coming Idol, ibid., October, 1880.

Protestant Church and Church-goers, ibid., July, 1882.

Labor Discontent, ibid., October, 1882.

*The Observance of Sunday, and Civil Laws for its Enforcement,
ibid.,* January, 1883.

Vagaries of Protestant Religious Belief, ibid., July, 1885.

What can be Done for the Orphans?, ibid., January, 1886.

The Church and Her Holy Days, ibid., July, 1886.

*A Pilgrimage to the Birthplace and Cloistered Home of Thomas
à Kempis, ibid.,* January, 1888.

The New Penal Code in Italy, ibid., July, 1888.

Wanted—A Textbook, ibid., October, 1888.

The Soldiers of the Blessed Virgin Mary, in the *Ave Maria,* May
3-10, 1890.

Our Lady of Prompt Succor, ibid., November 29, 1890.

The Latin Vulgate Civilizing Western Europe, in the *American
Catholic Quarterly Review,* for January, 1891.

Franciscans and St. Francis, in the *Dublin Review,* Vol. 92, p.
100.

Biographical sketches of Dr. Shea and estimates of his historical work will be found in the following: Appleton's *Annual*

Cyclopedia (1892); *Catholic News* (March 2, 1892), *Ave Maria*
(March 5, 1892), *Pilgrim* (April-May, 1892), *Catholic World*
(April, 1892), *Catholic Family Almanac* (1892), *Historical
Records and Studies* (U. S. Catholic Historical Society), Jan-
uary, 1899, and in the *American Catholic Quarterly Review* for
July, 1913. Cf. also Mode, *Source-Book and Bibliographical
Guide for American Church History,* pp. 296-314. Menasha,
Wis., 1921; *Catholic Builders of the Nation,* Vol. IV, p. 125, 323.
Boston, 1923. *Handbook of American Indians,* Vol. II, p. 1214.
Washington, 1912; and the *Catholic Encyclopedia,* Vol. XIII, p.
753-754 (Edward P. Spillane).